23

Conversational English-Nepali Dictionary

Sri Garib Das Oriental Series No.-86

Conversational English-Nepali Dictionary

Compiled by :
Anil Gupta

Sri Satguru Publications
A Division of
Indian Books Centre
Shakti Nagar, Delhi
INDIA

Published by :
Sri Satguru Publications.
Indological and Oriental Publishers
A Division of
Indian Books Centre
40/5, Shakti Nagar,
Delhi-110007
(INDIA)

First Edition : Delhi, 1993

ISBN 81-7030-377-X

PRINTED IN INDIA

ENGLISH	NEPALI
A universal monarch	Saarbabhauma
A beast's paw	Panjaa
A beaten track	Goreto
A big mouthed vessel	Baataa
A blast of wind	Phuinke
A carriage and four	Chaukade, Salebam
A carrying off	Haran
A change of form	Wikara
A chleftain of tenants	Mohenaaike
A curt and insolent reply	Othejawaf
A cut branch	Syaaulo
A cut-throat	Galkatta
A day's lesson in reading	Santha
A defunct person	Mritak
A detailed account	Phaatware
A different place	Sthaanaantar
A disguise	Bhesh
A down pour of rain	Darko
A drag net	Mahaajaal
A dry twig	Seto
A dwelling place	Rahane
A dwelling	Dham
A fallen leaf	Patingar
A fatal disease	Sannipata
A figure of speech	Wakyalankara
A great preparation	Dhumdham
A great quarrel	Sangralo
A group of birds	Bathaan
A group of villages	Maujaa
A handful	Gaas
A high pillar	Dharahara

A hymn of praise	Stotra
A jay (bird)	Thyouwa
A killing look	Katakchhya
A large open space	Patmaidaan
A leaf of the Bel-tree	Belpatra
A licentious person	Bhoktaa
A lie-abed	Sutaahaa
A line of huts	Taharo
A living being	Jewa
A lock of hair	Julfe, Lattaa
A long festoon of flowers	Toran
A long story	Ramkahane
A loose giving bachelor	Lutho
A loud calling	Sambodhan
A lump of ground pulse	Masyauraa
A lying-in-chamber	Rakshaagriha
A man of words not deeds	Phaasphuse
A mean person	Naraadham
A measure of contents	Bisaule
A measuring rod	Mandanda
A mesh of love	Maayaajaal
A middling pot	Bhujungo
A mixture of castes	Warnashankar
A mongoose	Nyaaure
A monthly publication	Maasikpatra
A mortar in which rice is husked	Dhike
A mound	Dhisko
A mourner at a funeral	Malaame
A mouthful of dry food	Phaak
A narrow passage	Bhanjyaan
A natural pool	Daha
A nearby ground	Lagaapata
A net formed by smoke	Moso

2

A *never drying land*	Sem
A *nose-pendant*	Bulake
A *peaceful state*	Raamraajya
A *person in disguise*	Bheshdhaare
A *petty ruler*	Rajawada
A *precipitious place*	Bher
A *primus stove*	Dam-chulho
A *rounding swing*	Rahote
A *safe place*	Aghach
A *sandy place*	Bagar
A *sermon*	Dharmopadesh
A *showy devotee*	Wakabhakaata
A *silly look*	Pakka
A *single fold*	Phankaa
A *sitting place*	Baithaan
A *solitary place*	Niraalaa
A *sore on the udder*	Thunilo
A *spiritual preceptor*	Dharmopa-deshak
A *spread sheet of accounts*	Rakamakalam
A *spring of water*	Nirjhar
A *stalwart fellow*	Lathe
A *state of disorder*	Lathaabajra
A *steep field*	Paakho
A *steep place*	Pakhero
A *stout young woman*	Patthe
A *sub collector's court*	Tahsel
A *suitable place*	Paahe
A *tailor's wallet*	Bukche
A *talkative person*	Phataro
A *tender child*	Sukumar
A *term of agreement*	Sharta
A *term of assent*	Lau

3

A term of respect	Baabusaaheb
	Mahaashaya
A thin crisp cake	Paapad
A thorough search	Dhuinpatal
A three legged chair	Tripaae
A tickling in the throat	Khaskhas
A tin alloy	Rana
A turning in the road	Mod
A twised cake	Ainthe
A two-pice bit	Dhyaak
A violent fellow	Hulyaha
A winding swing	Rotepeti
A winnowing fan	Naanlo
A woman having a son	Putrawate
A woman in child birth	Sutkere
A woman of low birth	Bajine
A word of praise	Shyaawaasa
A worthless fellow	Halambu
Abandoned	Warjita
Abbreviated	Sankshipta
Abbreviation	Sanchhepa
Able	Layaka, Samartha,
	Suyogya
Abortion	Adhigro
About	Lagabhaga
Above all	Sarwopari
Above mentioned	Purwokta
Above	Ubho
Abruptly	Chatakka,
	Pharakka
Absence of affection	Wirakti
Absence of distinction	Sarobar
Absence	Abhawa, Gayal,
	Nadarad

4

Absent	Gayab
Abundant blossom	Dhakmakka
Abundantly	Khalkhale
Abuse	Gali, Hapke
Academy	Widwatparishad
Acceptable	Grahya
Acceptance	Sakaara, Sahe, Swekaar, Swekriti
Accepted	Swekrit
Accessible	Sugam
Accidentally	Daiwat
Accomplice	Matwaalaa, Matiyaar
According to law	Widhiwat
According to	Anusar, Maafik
Account book	Dhadda, Syaha
Account	Khata, Lekhaa, Hisaab
Accountant	Bahedar
Accusation	Phatur
Acid	Teto
Acidity	Amalapitta
Acknowledge	Padkanu
Acquatic animal	Jalajantu
Acquisition	Phelaa
Acquittance	Bharpaae
Act of blowing up	Phukaai
Act of dividing	Bandaachundaa
Act of sinking	Dhasan
Act of splitting	Chiraane
Act of living	Rahanasahan
Active	Chanchal, Phurtilo, Sakriya
Activity	Tamak, Phurti

5

Actual	Yathartha, Waastawika, Sakale
Actuality	Wastawa
Adam's apple	Rudraghante
Addicted to crying	Runche
Addicted	Laggu
Addiction	Lata
Addition	Thap
Additional	Unau, Thapuwa
Address	Thegana, Pata
Adequate	Yatheshta
Adjective	Wisheshana
Administered	Shaasita
Administration	Raajapaatha, Raajya, Shaasan
Administrator	Shaasaka
Adolescence	Kukhurewains
Adoptedson	Dharmaputra
Adult	Praudh, Wayaska
Adulteration	Milaawat
Adulterer	Jaar
Advantage	Phaayadaa
Adverse	Wiruddha
Advertisement	Wigyaapana
Advice	Sallaaha
Advocate	Wakela
Aeroplane	Waayuyaana, Wimana, Wyomayaan
Affair	Maamalaa
Affected with gout	Bathyaahaa
Affecting the vital parts	Maarmik

Affection	Prem, Mamataa, Maayaa, Waatsalya, Sneha, Hittachitta
Affinitive	Sambandhe
Afflicted with goitre	Gadahaa
Affliction	Yantrana
Afraid	Bhaybhet, Daraaunu
Again and again	Waaranwaar
Age	Aayu, Umer, Jug, Bains
Aged	Budho, Wayowriddha
Agent	Gumastaa
Agitating	Manthan
Agitation	Aandolan, Wyagrataa
Agony	Kahar
Agree	Sojhinu
Agreement	Manjure, Sandhi, Samjhauta
Ague	Kamjwaro
Ailment	Wyaadhi
Aim	Uddeshya, Laksha
Air	Bataas, Wayu, Haawaa
Airy	Hawaadaar
Alarm	Khalbal
Alas!	Ha
Alcohol	Rakse
Alert	Chanaakho, Satarka
Algebra	Bejganit

7

Alive	Jiudo
All at once	Jhapakka
All naked	Nirbang
All of a sudden	Ekaek, Sahasa
All over the country	Bharmuluk
All rights	Sarwaadhikar
All seeing	Sarwagya
All-round	Chautarfe
All	Gairha, Saba, Sarwa, Saaraa
Allied forces	Mitraafauj
Allotment	Nikas
Allowance	Bhatta
Almond	Kagaje-badam
Almost	Pug-na-pug
Along with	Lagayata, Sameta
Alphabet	Akchhyar, Warnamala
Alteration	Pariwartan, Herfer
Although	Yadyapi, Hunata
Alum	Phatkire
Always	Sadaa, Sadaiwa, Saadhai, Hamesha, Harwakhat
Amazement	Chamatkaar
Ambassador	Raajaduta
Ammunitions & army	Lawalashkara
Amorous dalliance	Haawabhaawa
Amount	Rakama
An acquaintance with a form	Rupagyaan
An act of burning	Phue, Dhaakchhop
An act of silencing or hushing up	Thaamthum

An advance of money	Baina
An aggregate of five	Panchak
An almanac	Paatro
An altar	Yagyakunda
An animal's hole	Dulo
An ant	Kamilo
An appointed time	Miti
An arch	Gumaj
An archipelago	Dwep-samuha
An array	Waastraa-lankaar
An ascetic	Santa, Sanyase
An assemblage of microbes	Syaausyaau
An athlete	Malla
An atom	Parmanu
An atonement	Prayashchit
An auspicious day	Sudin
An auspicious moment for departure	Paaito
An auspicious moment	Sait
An auspicious song	Maagal
An earthern pot	Bhiut
An eel	Bam
An emerald	Pannaa
An eminent person	Narasinha
An empty begging	Tumade
An epic	Kabya, Mahaakaavya
An epidemic	Sarauto
An epithet of Durga	Bhagwati
An essay	Nibandha
An estimate	Adkal, Wajakhama

9

An exchange of beating	Lakapaka
An exchange of blows	Hanahan
An exclamation of contempt or rebuke	Dhat
An exclamation of pain	Aiyaa
An expansionist	Wistaarwade
An expounder of the Vedas	Brahmawade
An eyelash	Parelo
An initial learner	Sikaaru
An inn	Pauwaa
An insolent fellow	Hepaahaa
An irascible person	Phanfane
An island	Dwep
An itch	Aijeru
An oasis	Marusthal
An obedient servant	Tabedar
An observatory	Yantrashala
An offering to a deity	Wali
An open knife	Karda
An opportunist	Maukaawaade
An ostrich	Shuturmurga
An outward show	Phaainphutte
An ox	Saadhe
An umbrella made of sal-leaves	Syaakhu
An unchaste woman	Wyabhichaarine
An unexpected calamity	Bityas
An unwanted thing	Taaso
Analysis	Wishleshana
Ancestor	Purkhaa
Ancestral home	Kulghar
Anchorite	Saadhu
Ancient	Puraano, Prachen
And	Tatha

Anger	Krodh, Jhok, Risa, Risaane
Animal for conveyance	Waahana
Animal sacrifice	Hinsaa
Animal use in sacrifice	Yagya pushu
Animal	Janaawar
Animals food	Chaaraa
Animated being	Jantu
Anniversary	Waarshikot-sawaa
Ankle	Gole-gaatho
Ankles ornament	Paujeb
Anklet	Kalle
Annoyance	Dik
Annual	Barsene, Waarshik
Answer	Uttar
Ante room meeting	Baithak
Anti-aircraft	Wimaana bhede
Anus	Maldwaar
Anxiety	Udweg, Tulbul, Bhuto, Shok, Saksak, Sola
Any deficiency	Kasar
Any tree exuding resin	Dhupe
Anyhow	Kasai
Anything extra	Thapane
Anything given in charge	Naso
Anything spread out	Ochhyaaune, Bichhyaunu
Anything worn as a wrap	Odhne
Apparent	Pratyaksha
Appearance	Darshan, Mohadaa Warna, Huliya

Appeasing	Manaai
Appendix	Parishishta
Appetizing	Ruchikar
Apple	Syaau
Applicable	Lagu
Application	Darkhasta
Apply	Lepnu
Appointed	Bahaal
Appointment	Niyukti
Appreciation	Taref
Apprehension	Jhasko
Appropriate	Upayukta, Yathayogya, Yathochit
Approval	Angekar
Apricot	Khurpaane
April-May	Waishakh
Apt to anger	Risaahaa
Arbitrary	Chhanda-na-banda
Archaeological	Puraataatwik
Archaeology	Puraatattwa
Arched	Gumajdaar
Architecture	Shilpawidyaa
Area	Ilaka
Areca nut	Supaare
Argument	Chhalfal, Wiwaada
Argumentation	Wadawiwaada
Arm	Pakhuro, Bahaa, Bhuja
Armpit	Kaakhe, Bagal
Army	Phauj, Senaa

Arrangement	Intajam, Prabandha, Bandobasta Ryaanthyaan
Arrest	Dhadpakad
Arrogance	Abhiman, Sekhe
Arrogant	Abhimaane
Arrow	Kaad, Shara
Art of painting	Chitrakaare
Art	Kalaa
Artful	Pechilo
Articles bought in the market	Besaha
Articles	Saamagre
Artificial	Nakale, Banaawate
Artisan	Kaaligad, Shilpakaar
Artist	Shilpe
Arum	Pindaalu
As big as that	Tyatro
As big as this	Yatro
As far as possible	Yathaashakti
As if	Maano
As much as possible	Bharsak
As much as	Jati
As well as	Pani
Asafoetida	Hin
Ascetic renunciation	Wairaagya
Ascetic	Yoge
Ash	Bhasma
Ashamed	Lajamarnu
Asheath	Myaan,
Ashes	Kchhyaar, Kharane, Khaak, Raakha

Asparagus	Kurilo
Ass	Gadhaa, Sahaaya
Assistant	Sahaayaka
Associate	Sage
Associated	Sansarge
Astonished	Radda
Astonishment	Gas
Astronomy	Jyotish
At a single stroke	Chhatakka
At last	Akhir
At once	Turunta
At that very place	Uhen
At the back of	Pachhaadi
Attachment	Anuraag, Sanga, Chadhaai
Attack	Hamalaa
Attainable	Saadhya
Attendance	Tahal, Susaar, Syahar
Attendant	Tahaluwa
Attendants	Parijan
Attention	Chitta, Terpuchchhar, Dhyan
Attitude	Manobhaab
Attraction	Akarshan, Manpardo
Attractive	Hridayagraahe
Attractiveness	Hise
Auction	Lilami
Audience	Shrotagana
August-September	Bhadau
Austerity	Tap
Author	Granthakar

14

Authority	Adhikaar, Tainat, Butaa, Maathat
Autobiography	Aatmakatha
Autopsy	Lasajaacha
Awful	Bheshan, Rudra
Awkward situation	Jhamela
Babbling	yautyau
Bachelor	Kumaar
Back of body	Har, Peth
Back-biter	Chhulyaahaa, Khuskhuse
Backbiting	Bakawaad
Backbone	Dadaalnu, Dhaad, Mudh, Merudanda
Bad blood	Wairabhaawa
Bad character	Bajiyaa
Bad company	Kusangat
Bad conduct	Durachar
Bad habit	Kulat
Bad motive	Duragraha
Bad sign	Apashagun
Bad smell	Durgandha
Bad	Kharab
Badge of rank	Billaa
Bag of skin	Lota
Baggage	Jhitemite
Bail	Jamaanat
Balance	Leghro
Balcony	Ataale
Bald	Khalwat, Khuilna
Bale	Dhakar
Ball of the eye	Netramandal
Ball	Bhakundo
Ban	Manai

15

Banana	Kadaale, Keraa
Bandage	Patte
Banishment	Desh-nikala
Bank of a river	Ghat, Nadetat, Paneghat
Bank	Kinaar, Ter
Banker	Sarafe
Banyan tree	Baar
Barber	Nau, Hajam
Bard	Katthak, Gaine, Bhaat
Bare-headed	Mudulo
Bargain	Besaute
Barley	Jau
Barrel-shaped drum	Mridanga
Base	Pendh
Bashful woman	Lajjawate
Bashful	Lajjita
Bask in the heat	Tapnu
Basket	Bhakaare, Tokare, Dalo
Bastard	Haramjada
Batata	Suthane
Bathing	Snaan
Battalion	Paltan
Battlefield	Rangabhumi
Battlefield	Ranakshetra
Battle	Yuddha
Bayonet	Sangen
Be able to fly	Hurkanu
Be at one's elbow	Dhessinu
Be baffled	Hissinu
Be defeated	Latranu
Be dejected	Jhokrinu

16

Be destitute of ornament	Buchchinu
Be disobedient	Maattinu
Be down at full length	Lamchinu
Be drowned	Dubnu
Be famous	Kahalaunu
Be frightened	Dachkanu
Be furious with anger	Janginu
Be glossy	Talkanu
Be helpless	Thyoulinu
Be humble	Nuhunu
Be penitent	Thakthakaunu
Be pierced	Bijhnu
Be reddy	Kasinu
Be satisfied	Bujhnu
Be spoilt	Budnu
Be taken by surprise	Jillinu
Be uncertain	Dhalmalinu
Beads of rosary	Sumerne
Bear calf	Byauna
Bear fruit	Phalnu
Bear	Bhalu, Jhelna, Sahana
Bearable	Sahya
Beard	Dari
Beast	Pashu
Beat	Pitnu, Hirkaaunu Kutna, Thokna
Beating	Kutpet
Beau	Jhilke
Beautiful (of scene)	Ramaailo
Beautiful woman	Pare, Rupawate, Sundare
Beautiful	Darshaneya, Raamro, Sundar

Beauty	Aabhaa, Sundartaa Saundarya
Because of	Yasausale
Because	Kinabhane
Bechive	Polo
Become interested	Palkanu
Become	Hunu
Bed-bug	Udus
Bed-sheet	Tanna
Bed	Ochhyan, Bichhyaaunu, Bistar, Shayyaa
Bedding of grass	Sotar
Bedstead	Khat, Palan
Bee-hive	Ghaar
Beer	Jaad
Before	Agadi
Beggar	Bhikshuk, Bhekhmangaa, Magne, Yachaka
Beggary	Phakere
Begging	Bhikshaa, Bhekh
Beginning	Arambha, Uthan, Praarambha, Shuru
Behaviour	Wyawahar
Behind	Pachhiltira
Being as before	Yathaasthiti
Being without	Rahit
Belief	Bishwas
Believe	Patyauna
Bell-metal	Kaaso
Bell	Ghanta
Bellow	Dakaarnu

Bellowing	Dakaar
Bellows	Khalaate
Belonging to others	Biraano
Belonging to the second class	Doyam
Belonging to winter	Hiude
Below	Udho
Belt for the waist	Kandhane
Belt	Kammarpeti, Pete
Bending in old age	Kukrukka
Bending	Jhukan, Lachka
Beneficient	Paropkaare
Benefit	Labha
Bent of mind	Jhukaaw
Bent	Bango
Best end	Parmartha
Bet	Baaje, Hod
Betel seller	Barahe
Betrayal	Wishwasaghata
Better	Jate
Betting	Hodaabaaje
Big hole	Bhadkhaaro
Big	Saikala, Wirat, Ghwaak, Thulo
Bignosed	Nake
Bigotry	Hathdharma
Bilious humour	Pitta
Bill of exchange	Hunde
Bill	Bil
Billet	Lattu
Biography	Jewan-charitra
Bird	Charo, Pakshe, Pakheru
Birdlime	Liso

Birth day	Janmotsawa, Janmadin
Birth	Janma, Paidaish, Bhaawa
Biscuit	Biskut
Bitter experience	Handar
Bitter	Katu
Bitter bitumen	Shilaajita
Black-bee	Bhamaru
Black pepper	Marech
Black-tongued	Kaljibhre
Black	Kalo, Shyama
Blacksmith	Kau, Luhara
Blade	Dhar
Blamable	Nindaneya
Blame	Abagaal, Gafil, Gal, Dosh
Blanket	Paakhe
Blaze	Aach, Dhapakka
Blazing	Tantalapur, Dandanaudo, Prajwalit
Blessing	Asherwad
Blind in anger or pain	Ranthaninu
Blind	Andho
Blinded by lust	Kaamaandha
Blister	Phoko
Blood	Khun
Blood	Rakta, Rudhir
Bloodless	Raktahen
Bloody fight	Raktapaat
Blotting paper	Sosta
Blow	Ghuchchaa, Hirkaai

20

Blowing	Phunk
Blue vitriol	Nelotutho
Blue	Nelamme
Blunt	Dhetho, Bhutte
Blunt dugger	Syaatle
Blustering	Dhakku
Boasting	Dhak
Boat	Dunga, Nauka, Patelaa, Bot
Boatman	Maajhe
Bobbin	Lattae
Bodice	Cholo
Bodily strain	Dhapere
Bodily	Sharerika
Bodkin	Khapsiyo
Body guard	Hajuriya
Body	Gath, Deha, Cholaa, Sharera
Boil hard	Phatkanu
Boil	Umaalnu, Khatira, Pilot, Balkanu
Boiled rice	Maam
Boiled	Usinaahaa
Boiling	Bhulko
Bold	Abhaya
Boldness	Aat
Bolt	Chhiskine, Same
Bombardment	Bambad
Bond	Kabuliyat, Bhakhapatra
Bondsman	Gulaam
Bone	Hadde
Bonus	Phosaa

21

Book	Kitaab, Grantha, Pustak, Pothe
Boon	Prasaad, Wardana
Boot	But
Boring tool	Barmaa
Born	Paida, Jan-ma
Borrowing and lending	Lenadena
Borrowing	Sapat
Both sides of buttock	Philo
Both the eyes	Netrayugal
Both	Duwai
Botheration	Tanta, Phajete
Bottle	Botal
Bottom	Tala
Bottomless	Athaha
Bound Book	Jilda
Boundary	Dosaadh, Saadh, Sema
Bouquet of flowers	Guttho, Thugo
Bow	Dhanu
Bowl	Batuko
Bowman	Dhanurdhare
Box	Kantur, Baakas, Samput, Sandusa
Boxing	Bhanbhun, Mukkamukke
Boy	Keto, Ladako
Boycott	Bahishkar, Wahishkara
Boycotted	Wahishkrita
Boys and girls	Thitathite
Bracelet	Kankan, Churaa, Balo

22

Braggart	Gafe, Phaainphutte
Braid	Buttaa, Septe
Brain	Gide, Dimag, Magaj, Mathingal, Mastishka
Brainless	Buddhihen
Branch	Shakha, Haago
Brass vessel	Tasala
Brass	Pittal
Brave man	Marda
Brave	Nidar, Paraakrame, Bahaadur, Bor, Sahase, Himmatdaar
Bravery	Sahas, Himmat
Bravo	Dhanya
Bread	Charpate, Rote
Breadth	Gaj, Chaudaai
Break through	Pharnu
Break	Phodnu, Phornu
Breakage	Tod
Breaking	Phato
Breast	Thun, Wakshasthala
Breath	Daam, Sas
Breathing	Shwaasa
Breeze	Waata
Brethern	Bhaiyat
Bribe	Ghus
Brick-powder	Surke
Brick	Et
Bride-groom	Byahulo, Wara, Dulaha

23

Bride	Dulahe, Byaahule
Bridge	Pul
Bridle	Karele, Bagdor, Lagama
Brief	Chhotkare
Bright	Ujjar, Tejilo
Brightness	Kanti, Damak
Brilliant	Chamkilo, Panedar
Bring	Lyauna, Sagalna
Bristling	Romaanchit
Broad-sword	Tarwaar
Brocade	Kinkhaaw
Broken	Chaknaachur
Broken	Tutnu, Bhanga, Dalal
Brokerage	Dalale
Brook	Khahare
Broom	Khareto
Broth	Sup
Brother-in-law	Salo
Brother	Bhai, Bhraataa
Brotherhood	Bhraatritwa
Brotherly affection	Bhraatribhaawa
Brown	Khairo
Brownship grey	Phusro
Brush	Thakro, Kuche, Burush
Buck-wheat	Phaapar
Bucket	Balte
Bud	Kopilaa
Buddhist monastery	Gumbaa
Budget	Bajet
Buffalo calf	Paado

24

Buffalo heifer	Paade
Buffalo	Bhainse, Raago
Bugle	Bigul
Building	Imarat, Bhawan, Wastu
Bulb	Chim
Bulkiness	Badhaai
Bull calf	Bahar
Bull	Goru, Bayal, Bail
Bullet	Gole, Chharraa
Bunch	Guchchhaa, Jhuppo, Phuda
Bundle	Kunlo, Pulindaa, Bito, Muttho
Bungalow	Bangala
Burden	Bojh
Burial place	Chihan
Burn completely	Bhatbhataaunu, Rankanu
Burning ember	Philingo
Burning fuel	Balne
Burn	Balna, Jalna, Dadhna
Burning	Jalan, Daah
Burnt perfume	Dhup
Burst	Widerna
Bush	Jhaad, Buto, Mane
Business	Kaarbaar, Bepar, Wyaapaara
Businessman	Bepare, Wyaapaare
Busy	Kame
But	Parantu
Butcher	Kasae

Butt of a gun	Kunda
Butter milk	Mahi
Butter	Naune, Makkhan
Button	Taak
By means of	Dwara
By one's self	Swayam
Carten	Phard
Cabbage	Gobhe, Bandagobhe
Cage	Pinjara
Cake	Paurote
Calamity	Utpaat, Billabaath, Sankat
Calculation of price	Dardam
Calculations	Lekhajokha
Calf	Pindaaula
Call for help	Pukaarnu
Callipers	Parkaar
Calm and quiet	Saamasun
Caluminator	Bakawaade
Camel	Ut
Camp	Kampu
Camphor	Kapur, Bhemsenekapur
Canal	Nahar
Candle stand	Saamaadaan
Cane-mat	Maandro
Cane	Bet
Canine tooth	Kukur-daat
Cannon ball	Bam
Cannon house	Topkhana
Cannon	Top
Canopy	Mandap, Chaduwa
Cantation	Boksero

Cantonment	Chhaaune
Canvas bag	Namjo, Boraa
Canvas	Tat
Capacity	Taakat, Pain, Butaa
Capial	Jilo
Capital	Muldrawya, Raajadhaane
Capitalist	Punjewal, Saahukar
Captain	Saradaar, Subedaar
Capture	Pakad, Pakranu
Car	Motar
Caraway-seed	Jwaano
Cardamom	Alainche
Care of	Haste
Care	Jatan, Dhanda, Dhyaunna, Parwaah, Hifajat
Career	Jewane
Careful	Sawadhan, Hoshiyaar
Carefullness	Sambhar
Careless fellow	Hurdunge
Careless	Punman, Beparbaah, Bhuchchuk, Hoslyaan
Carelessly	Jathaabhuube
Carelessness	Laparwahe
Caressing	Laalana
Carpenter	Karme
Carpet	Galainchaa, Gajar

27

Carrying on the back	Bue
Cart	Gaadaa
Cartilage	Kurkurehad
Cartridge	Kaartus, Tota
Case	Khol
Cash	Nagad
Caste	Jat, Jati, Thar
Casting of vote	Matdaan
Castor	Ader
Castrated goat	Khase
Cat	Biraalo
Cataract	Chhaago
Catch	Pakrau
Catechu	Khayar
Caterpillar	Jhusilkero
Cauli-flower	Kaule, Phulkope
Cause of shame	Beijjate
Cause to be conveyed	Puryaunu
Cause to miss	Battaaunu
Cause	Hetu
Caution	Sawadhane
Cautiousness	Satarkataa
Cavalry	Risallaa
Cave	Odaar, Gufaa
Cavil	Mithyaawiwaad
Celebration	Ramarame
Celibatarian	Brahmachaare
Cement	Wajralepa
Cemetery	Shmashan
Censer	Dhupauro
Censure	Nindaa
Centipede	Kansutlo
Centre	Kendra, Madhya, Maajh

Ceremony	Samaaroha
Certainly	Awashya, Nishchaya
Chain	Janjer, Sanlo, Sikre, Seli
Chair	Kurse, Mech
Chalk	Kamero, Khare
Challenge	Pachkaarnu
Champion	Yoddhaa
Chance	Thau
Chandelier	Phanus
Change of direction	Ghumaai
Change	Adalbadal, Pherphor
Changed	Parinat, Wikrit
Channel	Kulo
Chapter	Adhyaaya
Character	Charitra
Charioteer	Rathe, Sarathi
Charity	Khairat, Dakshina
Charm	Jantar, Tuna, Tantra, Mohane, Laawanya
Charming	Manohar, Mohajanak, Laawanyawate
Chaste	Sate
Chastisement	Shaaste
Chastity	Satetwa
Cheat	Thag
Cheating	Thag-vidya
Cheek	Gala
Cheerful	Ujyaalo, Harshit
Chemical	Rasayanika

29

Cheroot	Bede
Cherry plum	Barro
Chess game	Buddhichaal
Chess	Bajaranga, Shatranja
Chest	Chhaate
Chestnut	Katus
Chicken-hearted	Chheruwaa
Chicken	Challaa
Chief commander	Mukhtiyaar
Chief of a monastery	Mahanta
Chief of a tribe	Thakale
Chief treasurer	Khajaanche
Chief	Mukhya
Child birth	Sutkero
Child	Bachcho, Laalaa
Childhood	Bachpan, Ladakapana
Childless	Aputo, Nihsantaan, Thare
Children's eating	Haam
Children	Ketaakete, Chhorachhore, Baalpothraa, Lala
Chilhood	Baalakkaal
Chilli	Khursaane
Chimney	Dhuaakas
Chin	Chiudo
Chinese plum	Lapse
Chip	Lopro
Chisel	Chinu
Cholera	Haijaa
Christian	Eshae
Chuckling	Khitkaa

Churning stick	Madhaane
Chutney	Chatne
Cicada	Jhyaukere
Cigarette-holder	Kulfe
Cigarrette	Churo
Cinnamon	Dalchene
Circle	Girdaa, Gheraa
Circuit	Phero
Circul	Ringai
Circular	Mandalakar
Circular array of troops	Chakrabyuha
Citizen	Naagarik
Citizen	Shahariyaa
Citizenship	Naagariktaa
City	Nagar, Shahar, Sadar
Civil court of law	Dewaane
Civil	Nijamate, Sabhya
Civility	Sohamat, Saur
Civilization	Sabhyata
Claim	Dabe, Daawaa
Claimant	Hakdaar
Claimed property	Bigo
Clappers of wood	Kathatal
Clapping	Tale, Thapade
Clarification	Spashtekaran
Clarionet	Kalaat
Clarionet	Shahanaai
Class-fellow	Paathebhaai, Sahapathe
Classical singer	Raage
Classical	Shastreya
Classification	Wargekarna
Clause	Upadhara

Claw	Nangro
Clay-pellet	Matyaangro
Clay	Matte
Clean	Shukla, Safa, Sugghar, Swachchha
Cleanliness	Shaucha, Safai, Swachchhataa
Clear	Nirmal, Sanlo, Spashta
Clearness	Spashtataa
Clenched fist	Ghussa
Clerk	Karindaa, Munse
Clever	Akkaldaar, Intelligent, Chatur, Chalaak
Cleverness	Chalaake, Bathyaae
Clever person	Bujhakkad
Climate	Haawaapaane
Climb	Uklana
Climbing-pole	Lisnu
Cloak	Daura, Mayalpos, Labeda
Clock	Ghade
Clod of earth	Chapare
Close confinement	Jakhadband, Najarbande
Close-fisted	Kirantoke, Chuiyaa
Close-fit	Timma
Close	Samaapti, Samepawarte
Closely	Jhandai

Clot	Phaalso
Cloth	Kapadaa, Panelaa, Lugaa
Clothes	Wastra
Cloud	Baadal, Megha
Cloudiness	Ruda
Cloudy day	Badale
Clove	Lawanga
Clue	Dase, Suraakh
Clump	Jhaag
Clyster	Pichkare
Co-education	Saha-shikshaa
Co-operator	Sahayoge
Co-wife	Sauta
Coach	Gaade
Coachman	Gaadaabaan
Coal black	Agare
Coal	Agar, Koila
Coarse and dry	Rukhasuka
Coarse	Phohore
Coat of mail	Kawach
Cob or pod of maize	Ghogo
Cobra	Goman, Saane
Cock-crowing	Kukhurekaa
Cock	Kukhuro
Cockatoo	Kakakul
Cocksureness	Dhukka
Coconut	Nariwal, Kopara
Coin	Tak, Sikkaa
Cold	Thanda, Thande, Sarde
Coldness	Shetalataa
Colic	Shula
Collapsed	Lutrukka

33

Collect	Jornu, Sametna
Collected	Saamel
Collection	Sankalan, Sangraha
Collector	Tahseldar
Collector's treasury	Tahbel
College	Kalej
Collision	Thakkar
Collyrium	Gajal, Surmaa
Colourfull	Rangabirange
Colour	Ranga
Coloured	Rangita
Colt	Bachhedo
Comb	Kainyo
Comber	Dhuniyaa
Come to one's sense	Jagnu
Comedy	Sukhaanta
Comet	Dhumraketu
Comfit	Laddu
Comfort	Phulyaunu
Commendation	Sarhaane
Comment	Tippane
Commentary	Teka
Commerce	Wanijya
Commercial house	Haaus
Committee	Samiti
Common to all	Sajiyaa
Common	Adna, Goswaaraa, Mamule, Larataro
Communal	Saampradayik
Companion	Sakhaa
Company	Kampane, Sangat
Comparison	Upama, Mukaawilaa

Compartment	Khaanaa, Dabba
Compensation	Bharna, Muaawajaa
Competition	Takkar, Pratiyogitaa
Competitor	Pratidwandwe
Complaint	Ujur, Nalish, Pukar, Phirad
Complete	Bharibharaau
Completed	Samaapta
Completely	Purnataya, Bilkul, Maremete
Completion	Purti, Pratishthaa
Composed	Rachita
Compost	Mal
Composure	Dherta
Comprehensive	Wistrit
Competition in bidding	Badhaabadh
Compulsion	Jhak
Compulsory	Aniwarya
Compunction	Pashchatap
Concentrated	Ekagra
Concern	Waastaa, Sarokaar
Concerning	Bare, Wishayaka
Conch-shell	Shankha
Conclusion	Upasanhaar, Khatam, Tamaame, Nidaa, Nishkarsha
Conclusive act	Chhedkhan
Condition	Dashaa, Haalat
Coneited	Dimage
Conference	Sammelan
Confess	Patkanu

35

Confine	Jaknu
Confession	Kaayal
Confidence	Bharosa
Confidence	Wiswaasa
Confidential	Wishwasta
Confuse	Labaryaun
Confusion	Bor, Hudalo, Ghabranu
Congestion	Kochaakoch
Conjunction	Sangama
Conjuror	Jhaakre
Connected	Narinu
Connection by marriage	Bihaabare
Conquest	Phatte
Contractor	Thekdar
Conscience	Antahkaran
Consciousness	Saatoputlo
Considerably long	Lammetana
Consideration	Marmolahija
Considered	Wicharita
Consolation	Dhadhas
Conspiracy	Shadyantra
Conspirator	Shadyantra-kaare
Constant complaining	Kachkach
Constellation (of stars)	Taramandal
Consternation	Haahaa
Constipation	Kabjiyat
Construct	Banaaunu
Consultative	Wichaaraadhen
Contact	Samparka, Sansarga
Containing a short vowel	Maatrik
Contemplation	Manan

36

Contemporary	Samakaalen
Contempt	Helaa
Contest	Jodtod
Continent	Mahadwep
Continuity	Parra
Continuous	Eknas, Nirantar
Continuously	Ektarai, Dhadaadhad, Pataapat, Bhakaabhak, Lagatar
Contortion	Batar
Contract	Thekka
Contraction	Sankocha
Contradiction	Bhanau
Control	Kabja, Washa
Controversial	Wiwaadaaspad
Controversy	Thakthuk
Convenience	Subistaa
Conversation	Kura, Batchet, Bolchaal, Warta, Wartalap
Convulsion	Chatpate
Cook	Pakaaunu
Cooking pot	Kasaude
Cooking	Pak
Cool	Chiso, Shetala
Coolie	Bhariyaa
Cooperative	Sahakaare
Copper plate	Taamaapatru
Copper vessel	Phose
Copper-vessels dealer	Tamaute
Copper	Tamo
Copulation	Maithun

37

Copy	Utaar, Nakal
Coral	Mugaa
Cord	Damlo
Core	Gubho
Coriander seed	Dhaniyaa
Cork	Bujo
Corner	Kuna
Cornered place	Soto
Cornice	Karnes
Coronation ceremony	Rajatilaka
Coronation	Abhishek, Rajyabhishek
Corpulence	Sthultaa
Correct	Durust
Corrected	Sanshodhit
Correction	Bhulsudhaar, Saste, Sanshodhan
Correspondence	Lekhapadhe
Corridor	Bardale
Corrugated iron	Karkat-pata
Corrupted	Bitlo, Bhrashta
Corruption	Bhrashtataa, Bhrashtaachaar
Crowded	Thasathas
Cost price	Paral
Costly	Mahago
Costume	Pahiran
Cosy	Nyaano
Coterie	Mitrasamaaj
Cottage industry	Gharelu-ilam
Cottage	Kute
Cotton	Kapaas, Rui, Ruwaa
Cottonny	Ruidar

Cough	Kaf, Khakaar
Cough	Khoke
Council	Mandal
Councillor	Sabhasad
Cunning fellow	Birsikhaa
Count	Gannu
Countenance	Ruparekha
Countermortgage	Lakhabandhaka
Counting the beads	Jap
Counting	Ginte, Nambar
Country	Desh, Pradesh, Muluka
Couple	Yugala
Couplet	Dohaa
Courage	Hute
Courageous	Sahasik
Course of events	Kalgati
Court	Kachahare, Nyayalaya, Wakaalat
Court notice	Samaan
Courteous	Winye
Courtier	Raajasabhaasada
Courtyard	Chok, Pataangine
Cover	Chhopnu
Coveted	Laalaayita
Cow's urine	Gaut
Cow-shed	Goth
Cow	Gae
Coward	Lachhe, Hikmathara
Cowardly	Darchheruwa, Naamaarda

Cowdung	Gobar
Cowry	Kaude
Crab	Gagato
Craft	Shilpa
Craftly	Dhutaahaa
Crane	Saaras
Craze	Sanaka
Cream of milk	Malaae
Creation	Nirmaan, Sirjanaa, Srishti
Creator	Widhaataa, Brahma, Srishtikartaa
Credit or debt of bet	Lagala
Credit	Shreya
Creeper	Bele, Bhyakur, Lataa
Creeper	Laharo
Cremation	Sanskaar
Cremation place	Masan
Crest	Siura
Crime	Aparaadh, Paap
Criminal	Paapaatmaa
Criminal court	Phaujdaare
Criminal	Aparaadhe, Paatake
Critical moment	Khatko
Crocodile	Gohe, Sos
Crooked	Tedho, Baake
Crop-eared ascetic	Kanfattaa
Crore	Kador
Cross beam	Bhaato
Cross-road	Chaubato
Cross-bred	Thimaha

Crossing over	Langhana
Crow	Kag
Crowd	Ludo, Ghuincho,
	Jamat, Dhuiro,
	Bhed, Bhedbhaad,
	Bhedaa, Relo,
	Larko, Hul
Crowding together	Thelamthela
Crown	Kiret, Mukut,
	Shiraposha
Crown-prince	Yuwaraaja
Crude	Kachchaa
Cruel	Amanushik,
	Nithur
Cruelty	Nirdayataa
Crust of bread	Maamre
Crust	Chhilko, Paapro
Cry for help	Duhai
Cry	Runu
Crystal	Phatik, Billaur,
	Sfatik
Cub of a bear	Gaddu
Cub of a lion	Damaru
Cuckoo	Koile
Cultivation of land	Abad
Culture	Sanskriti
Cucumber	Kaakro
Cumminseed	Jera
Cunning	Chhattu, Dhurta,
	Dhurtyaain
Cup-board	Daraaj
Cup	Kachaura, Pyala
Cupola	Burjaa
Curd	Dahi

Curds dish	Sikharne
Currency	Mudraa
Curry stone	Silauto
Curry	Kadhe
Curse	Sarapa
Curtain	Jhul
Curved	Wakra
Curvity	Wakrataa
Cushion	Baalista
Cusion	Gadde
Custard apple	Salifa
Custom-office	Bhansaar
Custom	Dastur, Prachaar, Prathaa, Riwaaja, Reti
Customer	Gahake
Cut tobacco	Kakkad
Cut	Chiro
Cymbals	Jhaajh, Jhyale
Dacca muslim	Dhaka
Dagger poniard	Kataaro
Dagger	Chupe
Daily wage	Majdure
Daily	Dinahu, Dainik, Rojindaa
Damage	Tut-fut, Bigaar, Haani
Damned	Chandaal
Damson	Aalubakhda
Dance	Nachaunu, Nach
Dancer	Natuwa
Dancing	Nritya
Dangerous	Phataha
Daring	Hyau

Dark red	Kaleje
Darkness	Adhyaaro
Darning	Rapfu
Date-palm	Khajur
Date	Chhohora, Tarekh, Tithi
Daughter-in law	Buhare
Daughter	Chhore, Putre
Day before yesterday	Asti
Day	Din, Roja
Daytime	Diuso
Dazzling light	Tirmir
Dead body	Murdaa, Lasa
Dead feud	Marnanta bair
Dead person	Moro
Dead-drunk	Tannaa
Dead	Mrita, Swargawaase
Deadly	Marubhumi
Deaf	Bahiro
Dear girl	Maiya
Death by hanging	Phaase
Death in general	Dehatyag
Death sentence	Mrityudanda
Death	Nirwaan, Mahaanidraa, Mrityu, Swargawaas
Debt	Karjaa
Debtor	Asame
December-January	Paush
Deception	Chhakkaapanjaa, Dhokaabaaje
Deceptive	Ghusghuse

43

Decide	Toknu
Decision	Tok, Nirnaya
Declaration of purpose	Sankalpa
Declaration	Marje
Decorated with designs	Butte
Decorate	Sajana, Singarna
Decorated	Wibhushita, Shobhit
Decoration	Shobhaa, Sajaai, Sajaawat
Decrease	Ghataaunu, Hras
Decree	Jetpatra
Deduction	Minaha
Deed of gift	Danpatra
Deed of trust	Dharmapatra
Deed	Karne, Bandapatra, Patta
Deep	Gahire, Gaadhaa, Mrigalochane
Deer	Jarayo, Mriga, Harin
Defeat in wrestling	Pachharnu
Defeated	Haruwa
Defect	Khot, Wikriti
Defective	Dokhaha
Defectless	Nishkalanka
Defence	Niwaaran
Defendant	Pratiwaade
Deficiency	Dyak, Hinta
Definition of a term	Paribhasha
Degradation	Maanbhanga
Deity	Dewa
Delay	Aber, Altal, Dhilo, Biyaalo, Wilamba

Delicacy	Narame
Delicate	Najuk, Phasko
Delight	Umang,
	Phurkyaahat,
	Rimijhime
Delighted	Gadgad
Deliverance	Uddhar
Delivery	Prasawa
Delusion	Maayaamoha
Demand	Chaaha, Maag
Democracy	Prajaatantra
Demon	Daanawa, Daitya,
	Betal
Demoness	Dankine
Dense thicket	Ghaare
Department	Wibhaaga
Departure	Prasthaan, Bida,
	Ramana
Dependent	Adhen, Prajaa
Deposit	Amaanat, Jakad
Deposited	Bandhake
Deprived of	Wihen
Descendants	Santaan
Descent	Oralo
Describe	Bakhannu
Description	Bistaar, Belebistar,
	Warnan,
	Wyaakhyaan
Desertion of a place	Uttha
Design	Baanke
Desire for companionship	Nyasro
Desire	Ichchhaa, Iraadaa,
	Kaamanaa, Taltal

Desired	Wanchhaneya
Despair	Hataash
Despatch	Chalan
Destitute	Tannam
Destroy	Bigaarnu, Nasnu
Destroyed	Dhwasta, Nashta, Barabaad
Destroyer	Widhwanse
Destroying	Widhwansakaare
Destructible	Nashwar
Destruction of the world	Mahaapralaya
Destruction	Bhransha, Laya, Wighatan, Widhwansa, Winaasha, Satyaanaasha, Sanhar
Details	Behoraa
Detective	Jaasus
Determination	Nidho
Devanagari script	Nagare
Development	Wikaasa
Device	Joho
Devil	Asur, Shaitan
Devoid of beauty	Shobhaahen
Devoid of taste	Beswaad
Devoted	Bhakta
Devotee	Tapaswe, Phaker
Devotion	Bhakti
Dew	Sheta
Dialogue	Samwaad
Diamond	Hera

46

Diarrhoea	Ukhaalpakhaal, Chheraaute, Chhernu, Pakhala
Dice	Tripaasaa, Paasaa
Dictionary	Kosh, Shabdakosh
Diet of fruit	Phalahar
Diet	Khuraak, Pathya
Difference	Antar, Pharak, Bhed
Different	Bhinna, Wiwidha
Difficult to cross	Dustar
Difficult to go through	Durgam
Difficult to manage	Ujjand
Difficult	Asjilo, Kathin, Garho, Jatil, Mushkil, Wikat
Digest	Pachaaunu
Digested	Pachnu
Digestion	Hajam, Pach
Digging through a wall	Nakabajane
Diligent search	Tadaruk
Dim	Dhamili
Din	Haura
Dining hall	Bhojnaalaya
Displeased	Nakhush
Direction	Dishaa, Nirdeshan
Dirt	Kasingar, Mayal
Dirtiness	Mailopan
Dirty-looking	Malin
Dirty	Phohor, Bhasar, Mailo
Disadvantage	Befaaidaa
Disagreeable	Beraje
Disagreement	Khadbad

47

Disappear	Alpanu, Dabinu
Disappeared	Bepattaa, Lapata, Lopa
Disappoint	Lopaarnu, Khissyanu
Disappointed	Niraash, Hissa
Disappointment	Ashabhanga, Niraashaa, Hares
Disaster	Apat, Bhawitabya
Disbelief	Awiswas
Discharge from monetary obligation	Phaarkhate
Discipline	Bandej
Disclosure of a secret	Pol, Bhandaafod
Disconnected	Chhutta
Discount	Katane, Kamisan
Discrimination	Pahichan, Bhedbhawa
Discussion	Bahas
Disease causing bald patch	Khoiro
Disease	Roga, Rogaahaa
Diseased	Lutyaangro
Disgrace	Bekadar
Disgust	Uchaat, Digmige
Disharmony	Bemel
Dishonest	Beemaan
Dishonoured	Beijjat
Disinclined	Wirakta
Disjunctive	Wibhaajaka
Dismissal	Nikalbaas
Dismissed	Kharij, Khosuwa, Jhikuwaa, Barakhasta

48

Disorder	Wiplawa
Disordered	Oltyanpaltyan, Khajyanmajyan
Disperse	Phinjnu
Displeased	Naaraaj
Disputation	Tarkana
Dispute	Kachingal, Tadkabaje
Disputed	Wiwaadgrasta
Disqualification	Awagun
Disregard	Niraadar
Disreputable	Durnaame
Disrepute	Durnaam
Disrespect	Anadar
Dissatisfaction	Nakhushe
Dissension	Phut
Dissolute	Chhaadaa
Dissolution	Pralaya, Bighatan
Distance	Para
Distant far-off	Tadha
Distort	Batarnu
Distress	Khed, Dukhaaunu, Durdashaa, Wiraha
Distressed	Pedit
Distributed	Witarita
Distribution	Bhagbandaa, Witarana
Distributor	Witaraka
District	Jilla
Disturbance	Upadrawa, Kachmach, Bakheda, Bighna, Hulhaal

49

Dive	Gota
Diversion	Dilbahar
Divided	Wichchhinna, Wibhaajita
Dividend	Wibhaajya
Divine knowledge	Brahmagyaan
Divorce	Tyaagnu, Pachuke
Divorced woman	Wiyogine
Document on the leaf of palm tree	Tadpatra
Dog	Kukur, Dhaap
Doing carelessly	Latyanpatyan
Doing so in anger	Ladebude
Domesticated	Paaluwa
Donation	Chandaa
Donor	Daataa
Door-frame	Chaukas'
Door	Darbaajaa, Dahilo, Dwaar, Pat
Doorkeeper	Dwaarpaal, Dwaare
Dose	Matra
Dot	Bindu
Double-edged	Duidhaare
Double-tongued	Duijibre
Double	Dochanda, Dobar, Doharo
Doubt	Dhukchuk, Bhram, Shankaa, Sandeha, Sanshaya
Dove	Dhukur
Down	Bhutlo
Downfall	Patan
Dowry	Daaijo, Pewa

Dozen	Darjan
Dragging along by force	Lachharpachhar
Dramatist	Naatyakaar
Drawer	Gharra
Dreadful	Bhayaanak
Dream	Sapanaa, Swapna
Dregs	Chokar
Dress	Basa
Dressing up	Singar
Dried and parched vegetable	Bhujare
Dried blister	Damro
Dried cow-dung	Guintha
Dried meat	Sukute
Drilling	Pareth
Drinking of wine	Madyapaan
Drinking	Paan
Drizzling	Rimarima, Simsim
Drop	Chhito, Bund
Dross	Jarte
Drought	Akaal, Bad-time, Untimely
Drugged	Lattha
Drugs	Jarebute
Drum	Dholak, Pakhaawaj
Drummer	Dholake, Pakhaawaje
Drumstick	Danka
Drunk (elephant)	Matta
Drunkard	Jadyaha, Matwaale, Botalbaaj
Dry ginger	Sutho, Munkkaa
Dry grass	Dhusnu

Dry tobacco	Surte
Dry	Obaano, Pasaangrinu, Burbure, Sukha
Duality in philosophy	Dwait
Duck	Hans
Due date	Myaada
Dull	Adhbesro, Uchatilo
Dumb person	Latyangro
Dumb-bell	Mudgal
Dumb	Lato
Dung of a cock	Lirhe
Dung of a horse	Lide
Dung of a mouse	Lenda
Dung of cock	Sule
Dunghill	Ghuraan
Duplicity	Chhal-chhaam
Durable	Akchhaya
Duration of three hours' time	Pahaar
Dust	Dhulo, Raja
Dutiful son	Saputa
Duty	Kartabya, Karma
Dwarf	Gathyaangro, Bhunte
Dwarfish	Baunne
Dyer	Chhipa
Dying	Maran, Maruwaa
Dynamite	Masalaa
Dysentery	Mase, Ragatamaase, Sangrahane
Each	Phe, Harek
Eager	Ichchhuk

Eagerness	Tarkhar, Dhoko
Eagle owl	Huchel
Ear pendant	Tap
Ear-pick	Kankarnu
Ear-ring	Gokul, Yarlinga, Karnaful
Ear-wax	Kaaneguje
Ear	Kan
Earliest	Agaute
Early in the morning	Bihaanai
Early morning	Praatahkaal, Bhor
Early	Jhismis, Saberai
Earn	Kamana
Earning by hard labour	Shramajewe
Earning	Arjan
Earnings	Upate
Ears ornament	Lwaanful
Earth	Jamen, Dharate, Bhuu, Mahe, Mato
Earthen pot	Hande
Earthen vessel	Arhe
Earthen water-pot	Golfu
Earthern lamp	Diyo
Earthquake	Bhuinchalo
Earthworm	Gadyaulo
Easily giving way	Phyaassa
Easily obtainable	Sulabha
East	Purwa, Sarala
Easy	Sahaja
Eat more	Dhadinu
Eat ravenously	Thesnu
Eat	Khana
Eatable	Bhojaneya
Eating	Bhojan

Ebb & flow	Jwaarbhaataa
Eclipse	Grahan
Economical	Mitabyaye
Economy	Pharo, Mitabyaya
Eczema	Ukuj
Edge	Del, Daate
Edible wild roots	Kandamul
Edible	Khaadya
Edited	Sampaadit
Editing	Sampaadana
Edition	Sanskaran
Editor	Sampaadaka
Editorial	Sampaadakeya
Educated	Shikshita
Education	Shikshaa
Educational department	Shikshaawibhaaga
Eengraving	Nakkashe
Effect	Asar, Ghat
Efficiency	Lyaakata
Effort	Utsaaha, Uddyam, Koshish, Cheshtaa, Prayatna, Yatna, Shrame
Egg	Phul
Eight of card	Atthaa
Eighteen	Athaara
Eighth day of lunar fortnight	Ashtame
Eighty-one	Ekase
Eighty-two	Bayase
Eighty-three	Triyase
Eighty-four	Chaurase
Eighty-five	Pachase
Eighty-six	Chhayase

54

Eighty-seven	Satase
Eighty-eight	Athase
Eighty-nine	Unannabbe
Elbow	Kuhunu
Elder brother	Daajyu
Elder sister of mother	Thuleama
Elder sister	Dide
Eldest	Jetho
Elected	Nirwachit, Manonit
Electricity	Bijule, Widyutshakti
Electrification	Widyutekarana
Elephant-driver	Maahute
Elephant	Hatte
Eleven	Eghara
Eleventh day in a lunar fortnig	Ekadashe
Eloquence	Waakpatutaa
Eloquent in speech	Waakpatu
Embarassment	Phasad
Embrace	Agalo
Embroidered with two colours	Raghepate
Embroidery work	Belbuttaa
Embroidery	Kaarchop, Battu
Emergency	Uparjhat
Eminent person	Shiromani
Emission	Udgaar
Emperor	Badshaha
Empire	Saamrajya
Employment	Rojagaar
Empress	Mahaaraane
Empty words	Wachanamaatra
Empty	Khale, Buchcho, Rittinu, Ritto

Encampment	Lashkara
Enchanting	Washikarana
Enclosure	Chhekaabaar
Encounter	Maarkaat,
	Muthbhet,
	Saamanaa
Encouragement	Protsaahan
Encumbrance	Ghaado
End of garment	Palla
End	Anta, Chheu,
	Jhwaya, Nihaayat
Ending	Wisarjan
Enemy	Dushman, Waire,
	Shatru
Energetic	Utsaahe, Jaagarilo
Energy	Jaagar
Energy	Saritaa
Engaged in a business	Wyawasaaye
English	Agreje
Englishman	Agrej
Engrave	Khodnu
Enjoy	Bhognu
Enjoying	Sokhe
Enjoyment	Upabhog,
	Bhogwilaas,
	Wilasa
Enlarge	Badhauna
Enmity	Dushmane,
	Dwesh, Waira,
	Shatrutaa
Enough	Kafe, Prachur,
	Bhayo
Enquiry	Puchhane, Sodhne
Enter into	Bedhnu

Enter	Ghusna
Entertaining	Manoranjak
Entertainment	Bhoj, Manoranjan, Winoda
Enthusiasm	Josh, Hausala
Enthusiastic	Joshilo
Entire assets	Sarwaswa
Entire	Tamaam
Entire	Saampurna, Saabut
Entrails	Lade
Entrance	Dyoudhe, Paithaare
Entwine	Chunyaanu
Envelop	Khaam, Lifaafaa
Envious	Dahe, Lubdha
Envy	Ekh, Dah
Enwrap	Lapetnu
Enwrapping	Lapetaa
Epidemical	Sankramaka
Epilepsy	Chharerog, Mirge
Equal age	Dautar
Equal	Baraabar, Sama
Equality	Samataa, Saraha
Equipment	Asabaab, Saajaabaaj
Era	Samwat
Erase	Puchhnu
Erect	Sojho
Escape	Suikuchchaa
Especially prepared work	Pharmaaish
Essence	Arak, Gude, Tattwa
Essential	Maulik

57

Establish	Sthapna
Established	Wyawasthit, Sthapit
Estimate	Andaaj
Estrangement	Mitrabhed
Evel-smelling	Jhisilo
Evening	Belukaa, Sandhyaa, Saajha
Every day	Harroj
Every means	Hartaraha
Every moment	Pratikshan
Every now and then	Jhaljhale
Every year	Saalbasaal
Every body	Sarwajana
Every one	Sabai
Every where	Jataatatai, Dhuindhuinte, Sarwatra
Evident	Prakat
Evil days	Durdin
Evil effort	Kucheshtaa
Evil inclination	Durmati
Evil omen	Alachchhin
Evil spirit	Pishach
Evil-smelling	Durgandhe
Ewe	Bhede
Exact	Thek
Exactly this	Yahe, Yai
Exaggeration	Atyukti
Examination	Parekshaa, Paarakh
Examine	Paarakhe
Examiner	Jaachake, Parekshak

58

Example	Udaaharan, Drishtanta, Najer
Exceedingly	Bichhatta
Excellent quality	Khupe
Excellent	Uttam, Khaasaa, Jharelo, Nokh, Badhiyaa
Except	Sibaaya
Excess	Bcsc
Excessive wrath	Prakop
Excessive	Upatta, Jyaastaa
Excessively	Dhum
Exchange of high words	Runkaranke
Exchange	Badalnu, Winimaya
Exchanging	Satta
Exclamation of alarm	Oho
Excrement of cattle	Bhakaaro
Excrement of goat	Barkaulaa
Excrement	Guhu, Wishtha
Excretion	Disa
Excursion	Sayal
Excuse	Bahanaa, Bingo
Executive officer	Subba
Executive	Karyakarine
Exemption	Maafe
Exercise ground	Akhaadaa
Exercise	Rafat, Wyaayaama
Exhausted	Hairan
Exhaustion	Hairaane
Exhibition	Tamaashaa, Pradarshane
Exorcism	Jhaarfuk
Expanded	Wikasit

Expenditure	Phaajil
Expense	Kharcha, Wyaya
Experience	Anubhawa, Wikshataa
Experienced	Paako, Budhopaako
Expert	Abhijnya, Ghagdan, Prawena, Sipalu
Explanation	Bakhaan, Bayaan, Wiwarana, Writanta
Explosion	Wisfota
Explosive	Wisfotaka
Exposed	Khulaa
Exposed to sum	Tattinu
Expulsion	Nikaalaa
Extend	Pasaarnu
Extended	Wisterna
Extension	Phaaj, Wistaar
Extensive	Brihat
Extent of a river	Pat
External	Wahya
Extra expenses	Phurmaas
Extra	Phaaltu, Phwaya, Badhtaa
Extravagant	Udantaa, Kharchilo, Phukaahaa
Extremity of a road	Naka
Eye	Aakhaa, Netra
Eyebrow	Aakhebhau, Bhrikute, Bhau
Eyelicl	Palak

Face	Chcharaa, Muhaar
Fact	Yathaarthataa
Factor	Bhajya
Factory	Kaarkhaanaa, Mel
Factotum	Hartakarta
Failure	Phel
Fair	Goro, Jaatraa, Melaa
Faith	Eman, Patyar
Falcon	Baj
Fall down	Dhalnu, Dhunmuninu
Fallow	Baajho
False witness	Mithyaasaathe
False	Jhuto, Nakaraa
Falsehood	Mithyaa
Fame	Kerti, Nekname
Famed	Yashaswe
Familiarity	Chinaajaane
Family priest	Purohityaain
Family	Kutumba, Kul, Jahan, Wansha
Famish	Bhokaimarnu
Famous	Naame, Neknaam, Prasiddha, Wikhyaata
Fan	Pankha
Fancy	Lahada
Fangs	Phanaa
Far	Pallo
Farewell	Shubham
Farmer	Kisan, Ropaahaar
Farming	Kisane, Khete
Fascinated	Mohit

61

Fascinating	Mohak
Fashion	Chalan, Thaat
Fashionable man	Sukulgundo
Fashionably dressed	Kasikasau, Sajisajaau
Fast	Ghanishtha, Wrata
Fasting	Anshan, Nikhalaam
Fat and tall	Labighare
Fat	Moto, Sthul
Fate	Karma, Tagder, Naseb, Bhaagya
Father's sister's husband	Phupajyu
Father-in-law's house	Sasurale
Father-in-law	Sasuro
Father	Pitaa, Babu
Fault-finding	Nindaacharcha
Fault	Kasur, Aib, Khaat, Chuk
Faultless	Nirdosh
Favour	Anugraha, Kripaa, Nigaaha, Nihoraa
Favourable time	Sahakaal
Favouritism	Tarafdaare
Fear apprehending danger	Jagjage
Fear	Atyas, Dar, Tras, Bibheshika, Bhaya
Fearless	Nirbhayaa
Fearlessly	Bedhadak
Fearlessness	Nirbhayata
Feature	Lakshana
February-March	Phaagun
Fee	Phes
Feeble	Nifar, Shithila

Feebleness	Shithilataa
Feel the need of	Parnu
Feeling great sorrow	Sokyaha
Feeling of sickness	Waakawaaka
Feeling	Bhaawanaa
Female ascetic	Yogine
Female author	Lekhikaa
Female cook	Adine
Female elephant	Dhoe
Female friend	Sangine, Sakhe
	Sahele
Female slave	Kamara, Dase
Female	Janaanaa, Mai,
	Stre
Fence	Bar
Fenugreek	Methe
Fermented juice of the palm	Taade
Fern	Unyu
Ferrier	Nalbande
Festal celebration	Chadbad
Festival music	Mangalwaadya
Festival	Utsawa, Chad,
	Parwa
Fetter for the neck	Galfande
Feudatory	Samante
Feverishness	Tapne
Few and far between	Jhakjhuka
Few	Ekadh
Fibre	Sutra
Fiddle	Sarange
Field	Kchhyetra, Khet
Fifteen	Pandhra
Fifth day of a lunar fortnight	Panchame

Fifth	Thaahilo, Pancham, Pachas
Fifty-one	Ekaunna
Fifty-two	Baunna
Fifty-three	Tripanna
Fifty-four	Chawanna
Fifty-five	Pachpanna
Fifty-six	Chhapanna
Fifty-seven	Santaunna
Fifty-eight	Anthaunna
Fifty-nine	Unsatthe
Fifty	Pachaas
Fight	Ladanta
Figure	Anjer
File	Reta
Filial devotion	Pitribhakti
Filing of a suit in court	Dayar
Filled with	Tanatan
Final beatitude	Paramgati
Finally settled	Thokuwa
Finance	Witta
Financier	Mahaajan
Find fault with	Phatkaarnu
Fine cloth	Tanjeb
Fine hair	Jhus
Fine wool cloth	Pashamenaa, Tosh
Fine	Masino
Finger ring	Authe
Finger	Angul, Aulo
Finish	Taya, Chukana, Siddhinu
Fire cracker	Patakaa
Fire lighted by a mendicant	Dhune
Fire place	Agenu

Fire spark	Jhilko
Fire-engine	Dam-kal, Warunayantra
Fire-works	Aatasbaaje
Fire	Agni, Ago
Fireplace	Borse
Firepot	Makal
Firewood	Daauraa
Firm	Daro, Dahro, Dridh, Dhruwa, Sthir
Firmness	Dridhataa, Sthirta
First-floor	Buingal
First	Pahilo, Pratham
Firstly	Prathamatah
Fish hook	Balchhe
Fisherman	Malaha
Fist	Mukkaa
Fit for a child	Bachkanaa
Fit for choosing	Roja
Fit to be separated	Bhedya
Fit	Daako, Murchhaa
Five colours	Pancharangaa
Five elements	Panchatattwa
Five kind of bread	Pachmel
Five	Pancha, Paach
Fix	Lagaaunu
Fixed look	Taktake
Fixed price	Nirakh
Fixed time	Muhurta
Fixed	Atal
Fixedly	Tulutulu
Flabbiness	Thalthal
Flag and banners	Dhwaja

65

Flag	Jhandaa, Pataka
Flame of fire	Lapko
Flame	Jwaalaa
Flannel	Phalaaten
Flash	Chamak
Flat	Chepto, Thepcho, Pate
Flattened	Chiuraa
Flattery	Khushamad, Molaahijaa
Flaunting	Nakale
Flea	Upiyaa
Flint	Darsan-dhungo
Flirtation	Maskare
Flirting	Nakharaa
Flood	Badhe, Bhal
Floor of an upper storey	Mataan
Flour mill	Jaato
Flour	Aato, Maida
Flow over	Pokhnu
Flow	Bahaw
Flower and leaf	Phulpaate
Flower-basket	Dhake
Flower-vase	Phuldaan
Flower	Pushpa, Phul
Flowerpot	Gamalaa
Flute	Wanshe
Flutter	Hadbad
Fluttering	Talbal
Fly-flapper	Chamaar, Makhauraa
Fly up	Udna
Fly	Jhengo, Makkhe, Makho

Foam	Phenj
Foeticide	Bhuranhatte
Fog	Kuiro, Hussa
Foggy	Dhumminu
Fold of a garment	Saro
Fold	Guna, Patal
Folk song	Lokageta
Following item	Tapsel
Following	Pechha
Fomentation	Seka
Font	Panchapaatra
Food and drink	Danapane
Food offered to an idol	Bhog
Food	Anna, Ahara
Fool	Swaath
Foolish	Durbuddhi, Nirbuddhi, Pamar, Bewakuf, Murkha, Latthaka
Foolishness	Kumati, Mudhataa, Murkhataa
Foot	Goda, Charan, Payar, Latte
Footstep	Paudan
For nothing	Khaainapaae, Sittai
For the sake of	Nimitta, Laage
Forbiddunce	Nishedh
Force	Jhakkaa, Bal
Forced labour	Begaar
Forcibly	Hathat
Forecast	Bhawishyawaane
Forehead	Nidhaar, Maath

67

Foreign country	Deshaantar, Pardesh, Mugalaan, Widesha
Foreign	Waideshika
Foreigner	Wideshe
Foremost	Sarwottam
Forest-fire	Dadhelo
Forest	Jangal, Wana
Foreword	Bhumikaa
Forget	Bhulnu
Forgiveness	Maaf
Fork of a tree	Kap
Form	Phaaraam, Rupa, Lifa
Formality	Retabhaata
Former	Bhutpurwa, Sabik
Formerly	Puraa
Formidable	Bhairawa
Formula for exorcising	Phakphuk
Fort	Killaa
Fortnightly	Pakshik
Fortress	Gadh
Fortune-teller	Jaise
Fortune	Daiwa
Forty	Chales
Forty-one	Ekhales
Forty-two	Bayales
Forty-three	Tritales
Forty-four	Chawales
Forty-five	Paintalis
Forty-six	Chhayales
Forty-Seven	Satachalesa
Forty-eight	Athchalis

68

Forty-nine	Unanchas
Foul means	Jaaljhel
Foul-speech	Lajabhaada
Foundation	Jag
Founder	Sthapaka
Four-legged	Chaukhutte
Four-wheel carriage	Bagge
Four	Char
Fourteen	Chaudha
Fourth	Kahinlo, Charau, Chautho
Fowler	Lubdhaka, Wyadha
Fox	Phyauro
Fragrance	Baasnaa, Subas
Fragrant flower	Kanakchampa
Frame	Phrem
Franchise	Matadhikar
Fraternal	Bhratriwat
Fratricide	Bhratrihatya
Fraud	Chhakaawat, Chhal, Jhel, Dhurtataa, Dhokaa, Phareb
Fraudulent	Dhokabaaj
Free action	Swechchhaachaar
Free from care or anxiety	Befikra
Free from desire	Wairaagi
Free from disease	Sarasaundo
Free from worry	Nishchinta
Free interchange of words	Bhanaabhan
Free of interest	Nirbyaje
Free will	Swechchhaa
Free	Swachchhanda

69

Freeze with cold	Gagarinu
Fresh cob of maize	Alauto
Fresh	Alo, Taajaa
Freshly tilled	Birauto
Friction	Sangharsha
Friday	Shukrawar
Fried	Bhtuwaa
Friend	Ishtamitra
Friend	Dost, Met, Yar, Sathe
Friendless	Mitrahen
Friendly feeling	Mitrabhaaw
Friends'	Jaafat
Friendship	Dostana, Doste, Mitere, Mitrataa,
Frightened	Jhasanga
Frightful	Darlagdo
Frigid	Kakrakka
Fringes	Jhallar
Frock	Nanaa
Frog	Paha, Bhyaaguto
Front	Morchaa
Frost	Tusaro
Frugality	Kifaayat
Fruit	Phal
Fruitarian	Phalaahaare
Fruitless	Nishfal, Wifala
Fruitlessness	Wifalata
Frustrated	Bokrina
Fry bread	Pure
Frying-pan	Tapke
Fuel for the sacrificial fire	Samidha
Fuel wood store	Khaliyo
Full grown youth	Bailhaa

Full of mud	Dabdabaudo
Full-grown she-buffalo	Thore
Full-moon day	Purnimaa
Full	Gamgam, Puraa
Fullness	Jhuse
Fully cooked	Paripakwa
Fun	Upahas, Thatta
Funeral pyre	Chitaa
Funny	Thatyoulo
Fur	Bhuwaa
Furious	Prachand
Furniture	Sarajama
Furred	Bhutlaawaal
Furrow	Dyan
Further	Pheri
Future	Bhawishya
Gain and loss	Chhwayaphwaya
Gain the victory over	Jitnu
Gain	Nafa, Praapte, Labdhi
Gainful	Laabhadaayaka
Gallop	Phal
Gallows	Shule
Gambler	Juwaade
Gambling	Juwaa
Game of fancy	Lahadwaaje
Game of hide and seek	Lukaamaare
Gap-toothed	Danta-dwaare
Gap	Phaake
Garden	Bagaincha
Garden mint	Pudena
Garden	Phulware, Baag
Gardener	Pagainche, Baagwaan, Maale

71

Gargling	Kulla
Garland	Maalaa
Garlic	Lashuna
Garment	Poshak
Garrulous	Phatphate
Gate door	Dhoka
Gate-keeper	Dhoke
Gathering	Bhelaa
Gautam Buddha	Buddha
Gecko	Maausule
Geneology	Wanshawale
General usage	Prayog
Generally	Aksar, Prayah
Generous	Udaar
Gentle	Bhadra, Sedha
Gentleman	Mahaanubhaaw,
	Mahodaya,
	Shremaan,
	Satpaatra
Gentlemanliness	Sajanataa
Genuineness	Wishuddhi
Geographical	Bhaugolik
Geography	Bhugol
Geometry	Rekhaganita
Get loose	Chhutnu, Jholinu
Get over	Taarnu
Getting tight	Surkane
Ghee	Ghiu
Ghost	Khyak, Bhut,
	Raake, Laakhe
Gibbet	Sule
Giddiness	Kahale, Chakkar,
	Bhaunna, Rengata
Gift of a cow	Godaan

72

Gift	Dan, Bhete, Saugaat
Gigantic	Ranaghwaka
Gilt	Jalap
Ginger	Aduwaa
Girl	Kete, Ladake
Give	Dina
Given to lying	Lawarchattu
Given to much study	Padhaiya
Given to much talking	Baturo
Given to pleasure	Aishe
Gladness	Danga
Glass	Kaach
Glimmering	Dhipdhip
Glorious	Prataape
Glory	Yasha
Gloubule	Bate
Glow-worm	Junkere
Glow	Tej
Glue	Saresa
Glutton	Ghichaahaa
Gnat	Piuso
Go beyond a limit	Naghnu
Go off in a huff	Bhankanu
Go to ruin	Bhatkanu
Goat	Chyangro
Gobbling	Kapaakap
God of Love	Kamdewa
God of Yamas	Yamaraj
God of Riches	Dhanpati
God	Eshwar, Brahma
Goddess of fortune	Kamala
Goddess	Dewe
Godfather	Dharmapitaa

73

Godless	Naastik
Godliness	Dewattwa
Goitre	Gaad
Gold necklace	Tilahare
Gold	Sun
Golden age	Satyayuga
Golden	Sunaulaa
Goldsmith	Sunaar
Gonorrhoea	Sujaaka
Good behaviour	Shela
Good birth	Gharaan
Good counsel	Hitopadesh, Sadupadesha
Good fortune	Swasti
Good health	Sancho
Good manners	Shishtaachaara
Good news	Mangalsamaachaar, Susamaachaar
Good omen	Subhnu
Good path	Supath
Good policy	Suneti
Good thoughts	Nekniyat
Good understanding	Sumati
Good-fortune	Shre
Good-luck	Saubhaagya
Good-will	Sadbhaawanaa
Good	Gatilo, Gahakilo, Bhalaa, Shubha
Goodluck	Chhuk
Goodness	Neke
Goods train	Malgade
Goods ware	Saudaa
Goonda	Gundaa

74

Goose	Rajahasa
Gorge	Khonch
Gourmand	Khanchuwaa
Gout	Baath
Government	Raajakaaja, Sarakaar
Governor	Haakim
Gown	Gaun
Grade	Klas
Grain-store	Dhansar
Grain	Anaaj
Grains	Kanika
Gram	Chanaa
Grammar	Wyakarana
Grammarian	Waiyakarana
Grand daughter	Naatine
Grand father	Dada, Baajye, Baabaa
Grand mother	Bajyai
Grand son	Nate
Grand	Bhabya
Grandfather	Pitaamaha
Grass	Ghaas, Trin
Grasshopper	Phatyaangro
Gratuity	Bakas
Grave	Kabra
Gray	Kailo
Gradually	Kramashah
Great anxiety	Ranaha
Great grand father	Barajyu
Great man	Bado
Great	Maha
Greatness	Badappan, Mahimaa

Great person	Mahaapurush
Greed	Laalacha, Lobha
Greedy	Laalache, Lobhe
Green colour	Jagare
Green straw of paddy	Naluwa
Green-fly	Didikero
Green-room the part	
behind the scenes	Nepathya
Green	Hariyo
Greenery	Hariyo-pariyo
Greeting	Namaskar
Grey	Tilchaawale
Grief	Aphasos
Grind	Pisnu
Groan	Hai
Groom	Chiruwaadaar,
	Saisa
Grotesque	Haasyajanak
Ground meal	Saatu
Ground pulse	Petho
Ground-floor	Chhinde
Ground	Bhaen, Bhuin
Groundless	Niraadhaar
Group	Warga,
	Samudaaya,
	Samuha, Upawan
Grown-up	Bainse
Growth	Badhte, Wriddhi
Gruel	Phaado
Grumble	Bhutbhut
Grumbling	Kachkache,
	Gangan

76

Guard	Athpahariya, Paharaa, Rakshaka, Lauka
Guardian	Sanrakchhyak
Guava	Belaute
Guess	Athot, Anumaan
Guest	Atithi
Guide	Aguwaa, Pathpradarshak
Guiltless	Bekasur
Guilty	Doshe, Bapate
Guinea	Ginne
Gulf	Khaade
Gum	Gud, Chob
Gums	Gija
Gunpowder	Barud
Gutter	Naale, Panaalo
Habit	Bane, Parej
Hail	Asinaa
Hair of the body	Raun
Hair-dye	Kalap
Hair	Kesh, Bal, Roma
Hairy	Jhusilo, Jhyaapjhyape
Half cut	Adhkatte
Half dead	Adhmaro
Half-dumb	Lathangro
Half-pants	Kattu
Half	Adhiya, Adhela,. Aadhaa
Ham	Saapro
Hammer	Ghan, Hatyaude
Hand-cart	Thelgade
Hand	Hat

77

Handcuff	Hatkade
Handful	Mutthe
Handkerchief	Rumala
Handle	Bcnd, Bedaa, Muth
Handsome man	Rupawaan
Hang up	Taagnu
Hanging	Latakana
Happiness	Sukha, Sokh
Happy and well-fed	Hrishtapusht
Happy	Khush, Prafulla, Sukhe, Hrishta
Harass	Padaaunu
Harassed	Aajit
Hard-excrement	Lindo
Hard-heartedness	Nithurtaa
Hard	Kadaa, Jarro, Sarho
Hardlabour	Dauddhup
Hare	Kharayo, Chaugadaa
Harmful	Hanikarak
Harp	Wena
Haste	Hatpat, Hatar
Hasty	Hadbade
Hat	Tope
Hate	Hiyaaunu
Hatred	Droh
Haughtiness	Tath
Having a piercer	Suire
Having a thin leg	Silakhutte
Having good taste	Rasika
Having irrgular features	Kopche
Having lost a limb	Dude

78

Having no address or place	Bethegan
Having no jurisdiction	Betaluk
Having no mouth	Nimukhaa
Having one's own way	Dhalemale
Having the desired effect	Saarthaka
Having the sad or	
sorrowful ending	Wiyoganta
Having tusks	Dataar
He,she,it	Tyo
He-goat	Bahhro
Head-cloth	Ghumto
Head	Kapal, Tauko,
	Thaplo, Manto,
	Shira
Headman	Thalu
Headstrong	Debro
Health	Swasthya
Healthy	Tagadaa,
	Tandurust, Nerog,
	Swastha
Heap	Khat, Dangur,
	Dher, Rasa
Hear	Sunna
Heart rending	Hridayawidaarak
Heart-touching	Hridayasparshe
Heart	Dil, Mutu, Hridaya
Heartfelt	Hardik
Heat	Tap
Heaven	Dargaahaa,
	Dewalok,
	Paramdham,
	Swarga
Heavily	Jhamjham
Heavy	Garhau

79

Heel	Kurkuchchaa
Height	Uchai
Heir-apparency	Yauwarajya
Hell	Narak, Yamalok, Patal
Hellish	Narake
Helmet	Top
Help	Upkaar, Guhar, Madat, Sahayata
Helper	Madate
Helpless	Bicharo
Helplessness	Bichalle, Laachaare
Helter-skelter	Chhyaannab-yaanna
Hem	Mohoje
Hemp smoker	Gajade
Hemp	Ganja, San
Hen-pecked	Joetingre
Hen	Kukhure
Herbs and drugs	Okhate mulo
Here and there	Yatratatra
Here	Yata, Yaha
Heroic deed	Paraakram
Heroic	Suro
Hesitating mood	Doman
Hesitation	Anakane
Hestoric	Aitihasik
Hiccough	Hikkaa
Hidden	Gupta, Chhipuwaa
Hide	Chhipaaunu, Luknu
High and low	Uchnech
High birth	Khandan

High prices	Mahage
High-mindedness	Mahatmya
High	Uchcha
Highest pleasure	Parmaananda
Highly pleased	Maganmasta
Hill partridge	Piuro
Hill	Daado
Hillocks and knolls	Thumkathumke
Hilltop	Thumko
Hinder	Pachillo
Hinderend	Puchhaar
Hindu code of laws	Dhrmasanhitaa
Hindu laws	Dharmashaastra
Hindu mythology	Puraan
Hinge	Chukul
Hip	Puttha
Hired labourer	Khetalo
History	Itihas
Hither and thither	Oltaa-koltaa
Hoar-frost	Os
Hockey stick	Girraa, Hakke
Hole	Chhidra, Chhed, Pwaal
Holi festival	Phagu
Holiness	Pawitrataa
Hollow of the palm	Pasar
Hollow	Khokro, Dhotro
Holy man	Mani
Holy place	Tertha, Punyabhumi
Holy	Pawitra
Homage	Paaulaage
Home of maternal uncle	Maawal
Homespun cloth	Khaade

Honest	Emandar, Nishkapat, Wishwase
Honesty	Jaman
Honey-bee	Maahure
Honey	Maha
Honour	Ijjat, Pardaa
Honourable	Maanneya
Hoof	Khur
Hook	Khep
Hookah	Gudgude
Hooting of an owl	Huhu
Hope	Umed, Bharos, Manorath
Hopeless	Laachara
Horn of Rhinoceros	Khag
Horn	Narasinga, Sen
Horoscope	Chinaa
Horrible	Wikarala
Horripilation	Romaancha
Horse-cart	Ekka
Horse-race	Ghod-daud
Horse-trainer	Sawaar
Horse	Ghodaa
Hostile	Dweshe
Hostility	Waimanasya
Hot-temper	Jhadanga, Tamtamahat
Hot-tempered	Janda
Hot	Ushna, Garam, Tato, Raapa
Hour	Ghanta
House of informal husband	Poil

House of lords	Bharadare
House-holder	Grihasthe
House	Ghar, Mukaam, Shala
Household	Khalak, Pariwar
How much	Kati
How	Kasare, Kaso
How much so ever	Jatisukai
Hubble-bubble	Hukkaa
Huddled together	Jhumma
Hue and cry	Kolaahal
Huge jar for storing grain	Ghyaampo
Huge	Ghanghor, Wishala
Human being	Manushya, Maanaw
Human	Maanawe
Humble	Winamra
Humbleness	Winaya
Humiliation	Maanhaane
Humility	Dentaa
Hump	Juro
Hunchbacked	Kupro
Hundred	Saya
Hundredth	Sayakada
Hunger	Bhok
Hungnail	Uchero
Hunter	Shikare
Hurriedly	Hatpate
Hurtful	Hinsaatmak
Husband and wife	Budhabuhe
Husband of elder sister	Bhinajyu
Husband of mother's elder sister	Thulobabu

Husband of niece	Bhanjejwain
Husband of wife's elder sister	Saadhudajyu
Husband of wife's younger sister	Saadhubhai
Husband's elder brother	Jethaajyu
Husband's sister	Nanda
Husband's younger brother	Dewar
Husband	Khasam, Naath, Pati, Poi, Pranadhar, Logne
Husk	Bhus
Hut	Chhapro, Jhupade
Hyena	Hapsilo
Hypocrisy	Aadambar, Paakhanda
Hypocritical	Paakhande, Swaange
Ice	Baraf
Idea	Bhawa, Mantabya, Wichara
Ideal	Aadarsha
Idiot	Gojyaangro
Idle talker	Gafaastak
If	Bhane, Yadi
Ignoble	Tuchchha
Ignorance	Moha
Ignorant	Gobar-ganesh
Ill-intention	Badneyat
Ill-feeling	Tus
Ill-fortune	Durgati
Ill-matched	Bijodaa, Bejod
Ill-repute	Baclnaam
Ill-shaped	Wirupa
Ill-will	Badkhwaain

Ill	Beraame
Illegal husband	Rakhaute
Illegal wife	Bhitrine
Illegible	Kirmire
Illuminator	Prakaashak
Illusion	Bhan, Bhraanti, Mithyaagyaan
Illusive	Bhraamak
Image	Murti
Imaginary	Kalpit
Imagination	Kalpanaa
Imaginative	Bhawuk
Imitated	Kachche
Imitation	Dekhasike
Immediately after	Bittikai
Immediately	Jhatta
Immensely rich	Malamal
Immersed	Lina
Immodest	Lajjaahen
Immoral character	Baclchalan
Immortal	Ajammare, Amar
Impelled	Prerit
Imperial throne	Takhat
Import	Magana
Import and export	Nikaascpaithaare
Important	Mahattwapurna
Impossible	Asambhawa
Impracticable	Asaadhya
Imprison	Thunnu
Imprisonment	Kaid, Thuna
Improper	Bemunaasib
Improve	Sadhana
Impudent	Thado
Impure	Khoto, Misaha

Impurity	Wyabhichaara
In a squatting position	Thachakka
In fact	Wastuta
In front of	Saamane
In good health	Changaa
In rough measure	Chhotomoto
In that way	Usare
In the absence of	Begar
In the middle of	Madhye
In these days	Haalsaal
In this very place	Yahen
In this way	Yastare
In which manner	Jasare
Inactive	Manda
Incarnation	Awataar
Incessantly	Dhamadham
Income tax	Aayakar
Income	Aamdaane, Kamai
Incompetent	Belaayak
Incomplete	Adhuro, Apuro
Inconsiderable	Jabo
Incorporeal	Niraakaar
Incorrect	Bethek
Increase	Badhna
Independence	Swatantrataa, Swaadhentaa
Independent	Saadha, Swatantra, Swaadhen
Indescribable	Akathaneya
Index	Suchepatra
Indicating mark	Wisarga
Indigestion	Apach, Badahjme, Mandagne

Indigo	Nel
Indirect rebuke	Ghurke
Indirect	Ghumaauro
Indis-speculation	Sakhtaa
Individual Job	Nijaayat
Indolent	Lome
Industry	Dhaamaa
Inexpensive	Sastro
Inferior in quality	Kamsal
Inferior	Ghatiya
Infinitive	Bhawawachak
Inflame	Jhosnu
Influence	Prabhaawa
Influenza	Rugha
Informer	Wigyaapaka
Initiated	Dekshit
Injured	Ghaite, Jakham
Injustice	Andher, wrong,
	Anyaaya, Julum,
	Bijaain, Beinsaaf
Ink	Mase
Inkstand	Masine
Inmates	Bhitriyaa
Inn-keeper	Bhattewaal
Inner courtyard	Aagan
Innocence	Bholaapan
Innocent	Ajaan, Abodh,
	Niraparaadhe,
	Bholaa
Inopportune time	Bemauka
Inquiry	Khoje
Inscription	Shilapatra
Insect	Kera
Insert	Hulnu

87

Inside of hand	Chapeta
Inside	Bhitra
Insight	Sukshmadrishti
Insignificant	Jhatingar, Nirghine
Insipid	Pachpachaaudo, Rasahen
Insipidity	Rasahenataa
Insistence	Dhipe
Inspiration	Prernaa
Inspite of	Taipani
Instigate	Uraalnu
Instigator	Karane
Institution	Sanstha, Arte
Instruction	Aadesh
Instructor	Wastaada
Insufficient	Kamte
Insult	Tiraskar
Insurance	Bema
Intellect	Pratibhaa, Samajha
Intelligence	Buddhi, Buddhimane, Wiweka
Intelligent	Jehandar, Tatho, Tekshna, Baatho, Buddhimaan
Intention	Abhipraaya, Neyat, Mansaya
Intercourse	Ratikam, Lasapasa
Interest	Chaaso, Byaj, Rahara
Interesting	Raharalaagdo

Interference	Dakhal, Hastakchhep
Interfering	Arghelo, Bingthyaahaa
Interpreter	Dobhase
Interrogate	Kernu
Interruption	Wighna
Intestine	Aat
Intimation	San
Intolerable heat	Bhabar
Intoxicant	Maad, Matyaaunu
Intoxicating	Maadak
Intoxication	Nashaa, Maste
Introduction	Parichaya, Prastaawanaa
Invention	Aawishkar, Rachanaa
Inventor	Rachayitaa
Investigation	Khojeneti, Taikat, Bujhbujhaa, Sukshmaparokshaa
Investigator	Sukshmapareksha-shaka
Invisible	Wilen
Invitation	Nimto, Bolaau, Bolaahaat
Invoice	Chalaane
Inward	Bhitre
Iron age	Kaliyug
Iron pan	Diure
Iron-rod	Dande
Iron	Istire, Phalaam, Lohaa
Irons	Nel

89

Irregular teeth	Chhwaake
Irrelevant	Andabanda
Irreligion	Adharma
Irreverence	Beadabe
Irrigation channel	Paain
Irrigation	Sinchai
Is it not so	Hagi
Isle	Tapu
Issue of step-mother	Sautane
Issue	Baalbachchaa
Isthmus	Ghate
Ivory	Hastihaad
Jackal	Syaal
Jackfruit	Katahar
Jackle	Bwaaso
Jail	Jel
January-February	Magh
Jasmine	Chamele, Jae, Juhe
Javelin	Barchhaa, Bhalaa
Jealous	Spardhe
Jealousy	Ibe, Spardhaa
Jerk	Jhatkaa
Jester	Labarapaade
Jew	Yahude
Jewel	Ratna
Jewels dealer	Juhare, Jawaahiraat
Joining	Yoga
Joint in bamboog	Aakhlo
Joint operation	Sahayog
Joint	Jorne
Joke	Khyaal, Dillage, Wyanga, Hasyaule
Journey	Sarar

90

Jovial	Nawarange
Joviality	Rasikata
Joy	Aananda
Judge	Dharmaadhikaare, Nyayadhesh
Judgement	Phaisala, Wiwechana
Jug with long neck	Surahe
Juice	Rasa
Juiceless	Phuko
Juicy	Rasilo
Jujube tree	Bayar
July-August	Shraawana
Jump over	Daaknu
Jumping	Phaad, Burkuse
Junction	Sanyog
Jungle-fowl	Luiche
Jupiter	Wrihaspati
Jurisdiction	Taluk, Laga
Just born	Laino
Just now	Bharkhar
Justice	Insaf, Niyaa
Justice	Nyaya
Jute bag	Dhokro
Jute	Nalu, Patuwa
Keen intelligence	Subuddhi
Keep watch	Runnu
Kernel of a coconut	Gare
Kernel	Raano
Kerosene oil	Mattetel
Kettledrum	Naumatebaja
Kick	Laata
Kid	Paatho
Kidneybean	Muge

Kill	Marna
Killer	Hatyara
Killing	Kattal, Mar
Kind-hearted	Mridul
Kind	Upakaare, Kaat, Kisim, Kripalu, Tarah, Dharmatma, Prakaar, Bhaati, Hitkar
Kindness	Daya, Paropkaar, Hit
Kindney	Mirgaula
King of Kings	Mahaaraajaa-dhiraaj
King's court	Raajasabha
King's crown	Raajamukut
King's representative	Raajapratinidhi
King	Maharaj, Raajaa
Kingdom	Raaja
Kingly	Raajase
Kingship	Raajapada
Kiss the ground	Lotnu
Kiss	Chumban, Mwaai
Kitchen-knife	Chulense
Kitchen	Pakshala, Bhaansaa, Bhojankhaanaa
Kitten	Nyaauro
Kitty	Bakkhu
Knap sack	Jhole
Knee	Ghuda
Knife	Khurpe
Knitting	Bunaai

92

Knocked away	Uchhittinu
Knot	Gaatho, Gujja, Bandhan, Surko
Knotty	Latapati
Knowing	Janne
Knowingly	Janajan
Knowledge	Thaha, Patta, Bodh, Widyaa
Known	Parichit
Known	Widita
Laborious	Parishrame
Labour	Parisram, Majdur, Shrama
Labourious	Mihinate
Lac	Lahaa
Lace	Jare, Pattha, Laisa
Lack of poverty of blood	Raktahenataa
Lad	Thito
Lady's finger	Ramtoriyaa
Lake	Jhel, Raha, Hrad
Lakh	Lakha
Lamb	Bhedo
Lame	Khorando, Langado
Lamp	Batte
Lancet	Nashtar
Land at the foot of hills	Tarae
Land held on rent	Raikara
Land-ownes	Talsin
Land-revenue	Uthatc
Land-slide	Oiraan
Land-tax	Bale
Land	Jaggaa, Thal, Bhumi, Sthal

Landed property	Tayadat
Landlord	Gharpatte,
	Jimedaar,
	Bhuswame
Lane	Galle
Language	Bole, Bhaashaa
Lantern	Lalatena
Lap	Kakh
Lapwing (a bird)	Hutityau
Large hearted	Dildar
Large hole	Todko
Large knife	Chhure
Large mosquito	Daash
Large shop	Kothe
Large	Lamme
Lassitude	Glani
Last day of the month	Masaanta
Last moment	Antakaal
Last	Aakhire, Chuttho
Lasting	Digo
Latch	Aglo
Late autumn	Hemanta
Late	Byaalo, Swargeya
Lateness	Ber
Later in the afternoon	Bhre
Later on	Pachhi
Latrine	Tatte, Paikhana,
	Shauchaalaya
Laugh	Haasna
Law suit	Mukadamaa
Law-court	Adalat
Law	Kanun
Layout	Meso
Lazy	Jumso

94

Leader	Naike, Neta
Leader	Mukhiyaa
Leaf cup	Bohota
Leaf of birch tree	Bhojpatra
Leaf of cassia	Tejapat
Leaf-cup	Duna
Leaf	Pat, Pato
Leak in little drops	Tapkanu
Leak	Chuhunu
Lean and thin	Khyaute, Chaaure, Dublo
Lean-bodied	Lure
Lean	Sikute
Learn	Sikna
Learned	Pathit
Least	Katti
Leather	Chamadaa
Leave	Chhutte, Tatel
Leaven	Daun
Leaves plate	Tapare, Patare
Lecture	Waktritaa
Ledger	Bahe
Leech	Jukaa, Khalepenaa
Left-handed	Bamkhutte
Left	Debre, Baya, Wama
Leg	Khuttaa, Taag
Legislator	Widhaayaka
Lemon	Kagate
Lending and borrowing	Aincho paincho
Lending	Paincho
Length	Lambaai
Lengthy	Lamcho
Lentil	Musuro

Leper	Kushthi
Leprosy	Kushtha, Mahaarog
Less	Kam, Manthar
Lesson	Path
Letter	Chitthe, Patra, Hastapatra
Lewdster	Randewaja
Liable to be damp	Osilo
Liable to be enwrapped	Lapetuwaa
Liable	Wyapya
Liar	Dhaat, Labara
Liberal	Phukkaa
Libertine	Phudo, Wyabhichaare
Library	Pustakalaya
Lid	Dhakne, Birko
Lie	Jhut
Life-estate	Jeune
Life	Jindage, Jewan, Pran
Lifeless	Nirjeb
Light green colour	Dhane
Light repast	Jalpaan
Light tiffin	Chamenaa
Light weight	Halka
Light	Chirakh, Chharito, Jyoti, Nur, Prakash
Lightning	Widyuta
Like a son	Putrawat
Like mad	Sillad
Like mother	Maatriwat
Like this	Yasto

Like	Tulya, Yathaa, Saman
Likely	Chhaat
Likewise	Yasare
Liking	Ruchi
Lime	Chun, Nibuwa
Limewater	Chunot
Limit	Maryaadaa, Simaanaa, Had
Limited by time	Myaade
Limitless	Apaar
Limp	Khochyaunu
Line	Taate, Dharko, Dharso, Rekhaa, Laama
Lineal succession	Parampara
Lines on the hand	Hastarekhaa
Linguist	Bahubhashe
Linseed	Aalas, Tise
Lion	Sinha
Liquid	Jhol
Liquorice	Jethemadhu
Lirs	Oth
Lisping babbling	Tote
List of words	Shabdaawale
List	Terej, Namawale, Suche
Listener	Shrota
Literary	Sahityika
Literate	Pandit
Literature	Sahitya
Litigant	Jhagadiyaa
Litter	Airelu, Khataule
Little boy	Naabaalak

97

Little children	Phucha-phache
Little girl	Balika
Little-finger	Kanchheaunla
Little	Ali, Ratte
Livelihood	Udarpurti, Gujaaraa, Jewika
Liver	Kalejo
Living creature	Prane
Living on charity	Tapre
Living thing	Jewat
Lizard	Chheparo
Load	Bhar
Loaf-sugar	Sakkhar
Loafer	Lamfu
Loan	Udhaaro, Rin, Saapate
Lobbery	Luta
Local custom	Deshachar
Local	Sthaaneya
Locality	Bhek
Lock and key	Talakunje
Lock	Taalcha
Locust	Salaha
Lodging	Dera
Loin-cloth	Kachhad, Lagaunte
Lonely	Nirjan, Sunsan
Long expeditious march	Dhawa
Long life	Derghayu
Long sighted	Derghadarshe
Long stick	Latthe
Long-eared	Lambakarna
Long-lived	Chiranjebe
Long-tail	Lampuchhre

Long	Dergha, Lambaa
Look at	Dekhnu
Look one's way	Parkhanu
Look	Herna, Drishti, Najar
Looking after	Sahyaara
Looking glass	Aina, Sheshaa
Looking	Herai
Loose woman	Phude
Loose	Khukulo
Lophophorus	Daafe
Lord Shiva	Pashupati
Lord Vishnu	Narayan
Lord	Prabhu
Lordship	Prabhutaa
Lorry	Lare
Lose one's temper	Jhadkanu
Lost	Gum
Loss of all property	Dhutemate, Wismriti
Loss	Kchhyati, Giran, Tutta, Noksane, Hinamina
Lottery	Chitthaa
Lotus Petal	Kamalpatra
Lotus-eye	Kamaline
Lotus	Kamal, Pankaj
Loud	Charko
Louse	Jumro
Love	Pyaar, Preti, Lada
Loveliness	Lalitya
Lovely	Lalita
Lover	Natho, Preme
Loving	Snehe

Low caste	Kujat
Low-lying land	Aul
Low-minded	Chhuchcho, Nech
Low	Necho, Hen, Hocho
Luck	Kismat
Lucky	Bhaagyamaane, Saubhagyawan
Luggage	Maaltaal
Lukewarm	Mantaato
Lump	Dhiko
Lunar eclipse	Chandragrahan
Lunch	Khaja
Lungs	Phokso
Lust	Unmaad, Laalasaa
Lustful	Unmaade
Lustre	Chahak
Lustrous	Chahakilo, Tejaswe
Luxurious pleasure	Aish
Luxurious	Moje, Rawaafilo, Wilase
Lying on the back	Uttano, Chit
Mace	Gada, Jaipatre
Machine part	Purjaa
Machine	Kal, Yantra
Mad	Unmatta
Mad	Paagal
Mad	Baulaahaa
Mad	Mattaa
Made of cotton	Sute
Made of felt	Jamoth
Made to order	Phaarmaaishe
Macle	Banana

100

Madhouse	Pagalkhaanaa
Madness	Paagalpan
Magazine	Patrika
Magic	Chatak, Jadu
Magician	Chatke
Magnet	Chumbak
Magnificence	Jhakijhakau
Magnolia	Champa
Maid	Kumare
Mail glove	Bholto
Mail	Daak
Maimed	Lulo
Mainly	Mukhyataa
Maintenance	Parwaste, Pushti
Maize	Makai
Maizecob	Khoyaa
Majesty	Pratap, Raajatwa, Raajasatta
Majority	Bahumat
Make angry	Chidhaaunu
Make cold	Selaunu
Make long	Lamyaunu
Make one's bed	Bichhyaunu
Make useless	Dhulyaaunu
Make wet	Ruhaunu
Making one's escape	Rapfuchakkar
Malaria	Aulo
Malarious place	Jhor
Male cat	Dhadc
Male	Purush
Malicious	Drohe
Man by man	Janahe
Man	Janaa
Management	Wyawasthaa

101

Manager	Wyawasthaapaka
Mane	Jagar, Yala
Manful	Nirdhakka
Mango	Aap
Mangy	Lute
Manhood	Purushatwa, Manushyatwa
Manly	Purusharthe
Manner of getting angry	Bhutukka
Manner of walking	Hindai
Manner or daubing	Latapata
Manner	Chaalaa, Dhab, Pranali, Reta, Widhi
Mannerless	Lwaange
Manners	Mijas
Mantlet	Lipto
Manured	Malilo
Manuscript	Hastalipi
Many-cloured	Bahurange
Map	Naksha, Maanchitra
Marble	Guchcha, Sangamarmar
March-April	Chait
March	Kuch
Margosa tree	Nem
Marigold	Sayapatre
Mark on the forehead	Tilak
Mark	Dam
Marked	Ankit
Market price	Bhaau
Market	Bajaar, Hat
Marriage procession	Janta, Bariyaat

Marriage-knot	Laganagaatho
Marriage	Bihaa, Wiwaaha
Married woman	Saubhaagyawate
Married	Wiwaahita
Marten	Malsaapro
Martyr	Shaheda
Marvellous	Adbhut
Masculinity	Purushjaati
Mask	Makundo
Mason	Dakarme
Massacre	Katmar
Master of the world	Jagatseth
Master	Sahewa, Swaame
Masticate	Chapaaunu
Mat	Gundre, Sukul
Match-maker	Lame
Match-stick	Salae
Match	Diyasalae
Matchless	Ajod, Dhurandhar
Materials	Saman
Maternal aunt	Maaijyu
Maternal uncle	Maamaa
Mathematics	Ganit
Matricide	Matrihatyaa
Matted hair	Jataa
Matter	Wishaya
Mature decision	Khatokhaat
May-June	Jeth
Meadow	Gaucharan, Chaur
Meal	Jiunaar
Mean	Naathe
Meaning	Artha
Meaningless word in repetition	Thego
Means	Gachchhe

Meantime	Madhyakaal
Measure	Naapnu, Mapnu, Pariman, Saache
Measurement	Napana, Nap, Maap
Measuring rod	Taago
Meat dealer	Bagare
Meat	Maasu
Mechanic	Mistre, Yantrawidya
Medal	Takma, Padak
Mediation	Madyasthataa
Mediator	Madhyastha
Medicinal gum	Mimiyaa
Medicinal plant	Sahadewe
Medicine	Okhate, Bute
Medieval	Madhyakalen
Medium	Madhyam, Saadhan
Meeting in session	Ijlas
Meeting of two roads	Dobaato
Meeting place	Addaa
Meeting	Bhet, Sabhaa
Melt	Galnu, Paglanu
Melting ghee	Bilaaune
Member	Sadasya
Membrane	Jhille
Memento	Yadagar
Memorable	Smaran-shakti
Memorial	Smaarak
Memory	Smriti
Men and money	Dhanjan
Mend	Tunnu
Mental agony	Manastaap

Mental sorrow	Santaapa
Mental	Maansik
Mention	Jikre
Merchant	Baniyaa
Merciful	Dayaalu
Mercury	Paaro
Merely	Phagat, Maatra
Message	Sandesha
Messenger of Death	Yamadut
Messenger	Dut
Metal alloy	Kaskut
Metal spring	Kamaane
Metal	Drabya, Dhaatu
Metamorphosis	Rupaantar
Metaphor	Rupak
Method	Kaida, Dhanga,
	Tareka, Paripaate,
	Roha
Mid-winter	Shishira
Midable	Maapaa
Middle finger	Maajheaulaa
Middle-aged	Adhbainse
Middle	Bech, Majhaula
Middleman	Lauke
Midnight	Madhyaraatri
Midwife	Sudenne
Milch	Duhune
Mild	Namra
Mile	Mel
Military	Jange
Milk	Bighaute, Goras,
	Dudh
Milk vessel	Gabuwa
Milkmaid	Gwaline

105

Milkman	Gwala
Miller	Ghatero
Millet	Kodo, Jai, Paandur
Millionaire	Kadorpati, Lakhapati
Mind and body	Tanman
Mine	Khani, Mero
Minister of state	Dewan
Minister	Amatya, Mantre
Mint	Taksar
Miscellaneous account book	Dhapot
Misconduct	Kuchal, Bckaayadaa
Misdeed	Kikarma
Miser	Kanjus
Miserly	Kripan, Khichchu
Misery	Naubat
Misfortune	Abhaag, Apatti
Misfortune	Dukha, Durbhagya, Bijog, Wipatti, Habigat
Mislead	Bahakaunu
Mismanagement	Gadbad
Miss	Sushre
Mist	Dhainso
Mistake	Galat, Chukna, Bhul
Misuse	Talamathi
Mix	Gholnu, Milnu
Mixed	Chhasmise
Mixture	Chhyasmis, Mishran, Sarabare
Mobility	Rawafa
Moderately thick	Layalo

106

Modern	Nawen
Modernity	Nawenta
Modesty	Namrata
Molar tooth	Bangaro
Molasses	Khudo, Gud
Mole	Kothe
Moment	Kchhyan, Chhin
Momentary glance	Jhalak
Momentary sight	Jaake
Momento	Samjhauto
Monarchy	Rajatantra
Monastery	Math
Monday	Som
Money lender	Sahu
Money matters	Damkam
Money-bag	Toda, Phaacho
Money-lender	Seth
Money	Dhan, Pattu
Monkey	Dheduwa, Wanara
Monster	Rakshasa
Month	Mahena, Mas, Mainha
Month of Shrawan	Saun
Month of Chaitra-Baishkh	Wasanta
Monthly payment	Mahinaware
Monthly	Masik
Moon	Chandra
Moonlight	Chaadane, Junele, Jun
Mop	Kucho
More or less	Thorbahut
More	Badh, Badhe
Morning	Bihana
Mortal world	Mrityuloka

107

Mortgage	Bandhak
Moss	Jhyau
Most beautiful	Ramaneya
Most intelligent	Pratibhashale
Mother of birds	Mau
Mother's sister	Sane ama
Mother-in-law	Sasu
Mother-o'-pearl	Sipe
Mother	Mahatare, Maa, Mata, Muma, Janmabhumi
Motherhood	Matribhawa
Mother tongue	Maatribhasha
Mother land	Maatribhumi
Motion of the bowels	Dasta
Motion	Gati, Chal
Motive of others	Laka
Motive	Ashaya, Prayojan, Matlab
Moulded	Dhaluwa
Mountain top	Dyaurale
Mountain	Parwat, Pahad
Moustache	Juga
Mouth	Mukh
Movable or immovable usufructuary	Bhogbandhake
Movable	Chal
Movement	Halchal
Much	Achkaale, Jyada, Dherai, Bahut
Mud	Ahal
Mud	Dabdab, Daldal, Pank, Repa
Muddy	Daldale, Dhamilo

Mug	Lohata
Mulberry	Kimbu
Multi-coloured	Chhirbire
Multiplication table	Dunot, Pahada
Mumble	Lakapakaunu
Murder	Wadha, Hatte, Hatya
Murderer	Jyanmara, Saidhuwa
Murderous	Hinsak
Murmur	Kalkal
Mushroom	Chyau
Music	Sangeta
Musical instrument	Baja, Wadya, Saj
Musician	Sangetakar
Musk rat	Chhuchundro
Musk-melon	Kharbujo, Tarbujo
Musk	Kasture
Muslin	Malmal
Must	Jarur
Mustard seed	Tore, Sarsyun
Mustard	Rae, Silam
Muttering	Lakapaka
Mutual agreement	Rajewaje
Mutual exchange of good-will	Dhogbhet
Mutual exchange of labour	Parma
Mutual exchange of looks	Dekhadekh
Mutual exchange	Sattapatta, Satasat
Mutual malice	Radho
Mutual pulling by the hairs	Luchhaluchha
Mutual recrimination	Doshadosh
Mutual	Paraspar
Myna	Maina
Myrobalan	Pancharas

109

Myrtle	Mehade
Mysterious	Rahasyamaya
Nail-cutter	Naharne
Nail	Kela, Nan
Naked	Nanga, Nago, Beparda
Name ceremony of child	Namkaran
Name of a lunar mansion	Rohine
Name or trace	Namnishan
Name, caste and address	Naunamase
Name-list of the group of villages	Maujyane
Name	Jas, Nau, Nam
Nanimous	Sammata
Nape of a neck	Ghichro
Nape of the neck	Ghuchchuk
Nape	Gardan
Napkin	Anguchhaa
Narrow	Saaghuro
Nasal mucas	Singhan
Nation	Rashtra
National	Rashtriya
National flower of Nepal	Guraas
Nationalism	Rashtreyata
Nationalization	Rashtreyakarana
Native	Deshe, Swadeshe
Natural	Swabhawik
Naturally	Swabhawatah
Nature of a beast	Pashutwa
Nature	Dal, Prakriti, Behor, Swabhawa
Naughty	Upadryaha
Near	Nagech, Najek, Nira

Nearly correct or exact	Motamote
Nearness	Pas
Neat	Safa
Necessary	Aawashyak
Necessity	Jarurat, Darkar
Neck bone	Mantethinguro
Necklace	Kantha, Har
Need	Khaacho, Garja
Needle	Siyo, Suiro
Neglect	Upekchhya, Helchakrai
Negligence	Gaflat
Negro	Habse
Neighbour	Chhimeke
Neighbourhood	Chhimek
Neighing	Hinhinai
Neither male nor female	Napunsak
Neither this nor that	Phussa
Nepale caste	Newar
Nepalese sword	Khukure
Nephew	Bhatijo, Bhanjo
Nervousness	Dhak
Nest	Gud
Net	Jal, Pash
Never doing again	Doholo
Never	Kadapi
Nevertheless	Tai
New shoot	Duku
New	Nayaa, Naulo
News	Khabar, Samachar, Halkhabar
Newsman	Patrakar
Newspaper	Akhawaar

Next	Dosro
Nib	Neb
Niche	Khopa
Niece	Bhatije, Bhanje
Niggardly	Lichada
Night duty	Bikate
Night-blindedness	Rataundhe
Night	Rata, Rate
Nightfall	Jhamakka
Nightingale	Jurele
Nine jewels	Nawaratna
Nine planets	Nawagraha
Nine	Nau
Nineteen	Unnais
Ninety-one	Ekannabbe
Ninety-two	Bayannabbe
Ninety-three	Triyannabbe
Ninety-four	Chauranabbe
Ninety-five	Panchannabe
Ninety-six	Chhayanabbe
Ninety-seven	Santannabbe
Ninety-eight	Anthannabbe
Ninety-nine	Unansaya
Ninth day of a lunar month	Nawame
Nipple	Stan
Nit	Likho
No	Nain
Nobility	Bhadrata
Noble family	Kulgharana
Noble man	Sajjan
Noble-minded	Pharasilo
Nobleman	Badaadame, Bharadar, Raesa
Noise of footsteps	Damko

Noise of wind	Hururu
Noise	Dhwani, Halla
Nonsense	Natckute
Nonsensical talk	Jhyaujhyau
Nook and corner	Kunakane
Noon	Dopahar, Madhyahna
North	Uttar
Nose-clipped	Nakato
Nose-ring	Nattha
Nose	Nak
Nostril	Poro
Not a little	Ekjat
Not admitting of further appeal	Beujur
Not bold	Lotre
Not in good health	Bisancho
Not	Hoina
Noted	Jaher
Nothing of value	Phasphus
Nothing	Phis
Notice	Ishtihar, Urde, Suchana
Notification	Wigyaapti
Notified	Suchit
Noun	Sangya
Novel	Upanyas
Now a-day	Aajkal
Now	Aba, Ahile
Numb with cold	Thihirina
Number	Anka, Sankhya
Numbered	Nambare
Numberless	Anginte
Numerous	Prashasta
Nurse	Dhae

Nurture	Palanposhan, Poshan
Nutmeg	Jaifal
Nutritive	Paushtik
O!	He
Oak-tree	Phalaat
Oath upon religion	Dharodharma
Oath	Kiriya
Obedient	Wafadar
Obeisance	Dandawat
Obesity	Motaapan
Object in view	Tak
Objection	Jirah, Wirodha
Obligation	Bhara
Obscene	Ashlel
Obscure	Dhamilyaunu
Obstacle	Chhek
Obstinacy	Adde, Tek, Hath
Obstinate	Dhinganyaha
Obstinate	Hathe
Obstruction	Paribanda, Bithola, Rokawata
Obtained	Wasula, Hasil
Occasion	Jog, Mauka
Occupation	Uddyog, Kamkaj, Dhandha, Pesha, Wyawasaaya
Ocean	Mahaa Sagar
Ochre-coloured	Geruwa
Octroi duty	Chunge
Odd numbers	Bijor
Odd jobs	Tanemane
Of a different colour	Bhinnawarna
Of a hand's length	Ekhate

114

Of a small stature	Pudko
Of different caste	Wijaatiya
Of entirely	Nikhur
Of loose morals	Bhrashtaachaare
Of mixed blood	Khachchad
Of noble family	Kulen, Gharaniyaa
Of one mind	Sahamat
Of opposite nature	Debro
Of several fashions	Naurange
Of the intellect	Bauddhik
Of the nature of unmindful	Jarkato
Of the nature of unproductive	Jimaha
Of the same age	Dautare
Of two colours	Doranga, Raghe
Of what kind	Kasto
Offence	Patak
Offer	Chadhaunu
Offering of flowers	Pushpanjale
Offering water	Argha
Offering	Aahuti
Official	Adhikaare
Office	Daftar
Officer	Padadhikare
Official letter	Rukka
Officiating	Kayammukayam
Ogling	Masakka
Oil dealer	Salme
Oil man	Tele
Oil-cake	Pina
Oil-press	Kol
Oil	Tel
Oily and glossy brick	Teliyaent
Oily	Chillo
Ointment	Malham

Old age	Wriddhawastha
Old lady	Budhe
Old worn-out	Phyanlo
Old	Thotro, Wriddha
Omen	Shakun, Saguna
On both sides	Warepare
On foot	Paidal
On the average	Saalaakhaalaa
On the morrow	Bholipalta
On the other hand	Utaa
On the other side	Pare
On this side or that	Waarpaar
On this side	Waare
Once	Ekjhamat
One and a half	Dedh
One and a quarter	Sawai
One anna bit	Ekanne
One by one	Pichchhe
One copy	Prati
One day and night	Raatadina
One devoted to luxury	Bhoglolup
One forth	Pau
One fourth of a rupee	Suka, Kanuwa
One given or prone to falsehood	Dhatuwa
One gulp	Ghutko
One man's work	Laga
One meal	Chhak
One of the eighteen Puranas	Bhaagwat
One only	Ekota
One who accepts bribe	Ghusyaha
One who carries	Bokaahaa
One who earns	Kamasut
One who enjoys a thing	Bhoge

116

One who is versed in sacred lore	Shastre
One who keeps accounts	Rakame
One who lives alone	Ekantawase
One who makes a selection	Nirwachak
One who performs a sacrifice	Yajaman
One who sells charcoal	Gole
One who shirks one's work	Kaamchor
One who stands surety	Dhanjamaane
One who takes	Hartaa
One's all	Tadetumade
One's equal	Jorepare
One's level best	Bharmagdur
One's own business	Swakaarya
One's own man	Swajan
One's own	Sakha, Swakeya
One-eyed	Kana
One-fold	Eksaro
One-fourth	Chauthai
One-sided	Ektarfe
One	Ek, Yauta
Onion like plant	Chhyape
Onion	Pyaj
Only	Khale
Ony by one	Phutphut
Open field	Maidaan
Open part of a market	Dabale
Open space in front of house	Baranda
Open	Khulasta, Phukuwa
Opening	Udghaatan
Openly	Khasaakhas, Hakahake

Opinion	Thyaak, Mat, Mato, Raya
Opponent	Wipakshe, Wirodhe, Samayochit
Opportunity	Dau
Opposed	Warkhilafa
Opposite	Ulta, Pratikul, Wipareta
Oppression	Thichomicho
Or	Athawa, Ki, Ya
Oral	Maukhik
Orange	Suntala
Order	Thiti, Paramange
Ordinarily	Saamaanyataa
Ordinary	Saadharana, Saamaanya
Organisation	Sangathana
Organised	Sangathit
Origin	Utpatti, Yoni, Wyutpati
Original copy	Gurukape
Original	Sadde
Ornament	Alankaar, Gahanaa, Bhushan, Shringar
Ornamented	Singare
Orphan	Tuhuro
Orthodox	Kattar
Orthography	Warnawichaar
Other countries	Deshawar
Other world	Paralok
Other	Aru, Parae
Otherwise	Natra

Otto	Lewendara
Our	Hamro
Out of tune	Besur
Outcast	Patit
Outside	Baahira
Outsider	Pardeshe
Outspoken	Chhicharo, Spashtawaktaa
Over crowded	Khachit
Over-power	Dabaunu
Over	Maathi
Overempowered	Washebhuta
Overjoyed	Dangadaas, Phurunga
Overwhelmed	Udwigna
Owing to	Hunaale
Owl	Ullu, Latokosero
Owner	Malik
Pack	Gunta
Package	Poko
Packet	Muturo
Padded bedding	Dasana
Paddy	Wangra
Page	Pana
Pain	Kashta, Darda, Per, Baha, Wedana
Painter	Chitrakaar
Plaintiff	Waacle
Pair	Jodaa, Dwanda
Palace	Darbar, Mahal
Palanquin-bearers	Kahar
Palanquin	Palake, Myaanaa
Palate	Talu
Palm of the hand	Hatkelo

119

Palm tree	Tad
Palpitation of the heart	Dhadak
Palpitation	Dhukdhuke
Pamphlet	Pustika
Pan	Tapes
Pandanus	Ketke
Pander	Bhanduwa
Panic	Attinu, Hahakar
Panther	Chituwa
Pants	Chusta
Papaya	Mewa
Paper money	Not
Paper slip	Purje
Paper	Kagat
Papya fruit	Papita
Parable	Ukhan, Kawaj
Paragraph	Parichchhed
Parallel	Samanantar
Paralyzed	Kathangri
Paramour	Upapati
Parasite	Bhate
Parcel	Paarsal
Parched rice	Khatte, Lawa
Pardon	Kchhyamaa
Parliament house	Sadan
Parrot	Sugaa
Part	Ansha, Portion, Khanda
Partiality	Pakshapat
Partition	Banda
Partner	Bhaage, Hissadar
Partnership	Saajaa
Partridge	Titro
Party	Dal

Pass away	Marnu
Pass one's life	Bitnu
Pass through	Chhicholnu
Passenger	Pathik, Yatre
Passing from one hand to another	Hathutgarera
Passive resistant	Satyagrahe
Passive	Nishkriya
Passport	Rahadane
Past generation	Parapurwa
Past	Gat, Wigat
Pasture	Kharka
Pat	Dhap
Patch	Talo
Paternal great grandfather	Prapitamaha
Path	Marga
Patience	Khaamas, Gam, Dhairya
Patient	Dher
Patrol	Ramana
Pause	Biram, Wirama
Pay more	Badhkaraar
Paying off	Bemakh
Payment in full	Chukte, Bhuktaan
Payment	Tiro
Pea	Matar
Peace	Shaanti
Peach	Aru
Peacock	Mujura
Peak of a mountain	Leka
Peak	Chule
Pear	Naspate
Pearl	Mote
Peas	Kerau

Pebble	Kankad
Pedlar	Upariya
Peeled	Tachhuwa
Peg	Khute
Pelletbow	Gulele
Pen-case	Kalamdan
Pen-knife	Chakku
Pen	Kalam, Lekhane
Penalty	Jarewana
Pencil	Sheshakalam
Pendulum	Langura
Peninsula	Prayadwep
Penitence	Thakthak, Pachhutau, Patiya
Pensioner	Bhattawal
Penurious	Tanaha
People	Duniya, Janata
Perception	Gochar
Perfumed	Sugandhit
Perhaps	Kadachit, Hola
Period of appointed time	Bhaakhaakhaawaa
Period of youth	Yuwawastha
Permanent	Sthaye
Permission	Agyaa
Perplexed	Bilakhbanda, Wyagra, Wyaakula, Wyaakulit
Perplexity	Dothyan, Rangeto, Wyaakulata
Person	Jana, Wyakti
Personal	Nije
Personality	Wyaktitwa, Khud
Pertaining to Buddhism	Bauddha

Pertaining to both the parties	Dohare
Pertaining to the court	Darbariya
Pervading the Universe	Wishwawyape
Pestle	Luse, Musal
Petition	Pintepatra
Pewter	Jasta
Phaeton	Phitan
Phantasmic	Maayaawe
Pheasant	Kalij
Phenol	Phinel
Phenomenon	Ulka
Photo	Taswer
Phthisis	Kchhyayarog
Physical exercise	Kasrat
Physical health	Tanduruste
Physical labour	Tandehe
Physical strength	Mudhebal
Physical	Bhautik
Physician	Waidya
Pickles	Achaar
Pickpocket	Pagalemara
Picture	Chitraa, Pratima
Piece	Choitaa, Tukra, Phyaak
Pig	Sugur
Pigeon	Lakka, Parewa, Haleso
Pile	Thele, Thupro
Piles	Alkae
Pilferer	Taptipe
Pilgrim	Jatru
Pill	Bare
Pillar	Khamba, Tham, Maulo, Stambha

Pillow	Takiya, Sirhan
Pimple	Bimiro
Pimples	Dadifor
Pincers	Sanaso
Pinch	Chukte
Pindrop silence	Chakmanna
Pine tree	Diyalo, Sallo
Pine-apple	Bhaenkatahar
Pine-cone	Simta
Pious	Bhadrashel
Pipe of a hubble-bubble	Naicha
Pipe	Nale, Ben, Phutte
Piquant	Ramarama
Pistachio nut	Pista
Pit	Khadal
Pitch	Alkatraa
Pitcher	Ghada
Place for burning the dead body	Masan
Place of pilgrimage	Dewatertha
Place of residence	That
Place	Sthan
Plague	Pleg, Mahamare
Plain	Sadha
Plaited hair	Chultho
Plan	Upaya, Jukti, Tarjuma, Yojana
Plains	Madhes
Plane	Randa
Planet Neptune	Nepchun
Planet	Graha
Plank	Phalek
Plant	Biruwa
Plaster	Lepa

Plate	Thal, Rikabe
Platform	Chautaro, Machaan
Play	Khel, Naatak, Lela
Player	Khelade
Playing card	Tash
Playing on a musical instrument	Waadana
Playing the fool	Swan
Plaything	Khelanche
Pleased	Magan, Raje
Pleasure	Aamod, Majaa
Pledge	Kabul
Plenty of food	Bhater
Plenty	Ghanera, Pawal, Bharmaar
Plethora	Raktapitta
Ploddingly	Suru-suru
Plough	Jotnu, Hal, Halo
Ploughing	Jot
Ploughshare	Phale
Plumbline	Saadhane
Plume	Kalke
Plummet	Saahul
Plump and fat	Motoghaato
Plump and stout	Thammarthummar
Plunder	Lutnu
Plunge	Dubulke
Pock-marked	Chhyakate
Pocket	Khalte, Jeb, Bagale
Pod	Bungo
Poem	Kawitaa
Poet	Kawi

Poetry	Padya
Point by name	Pargelnu
Point	Nok
Poison	Jahar, Wisha, Sankhiya
Poisonous	Wishalu
Polar star	Dhruwatara
Pole of a plough	Hares
Pole	Gharo, Lattha
Police station	Thana
Police sub-station	Chauke
Police-constable	Pulis
Policy	Neti
Polish	Palish
Polite	Sushel
Political	Raajanaitika
Politician	Netigyan, Raajanetigya
Politics	Raajaneti
Pomegranate	Daarim
Pond	Talau, Pokhare, Sarowar
Pony	Tattu, Taagan
Pool of spilt water	Pokharo
Pool	Tal
Poor condition	Bihal
Poor	Kangal, Gareb, Tangin, Daridra, Nirdhan, Phugin, Baburo, Bara
Popular saying	Lokokti
Popular	Sarwapriya
Populated	Guljar
Porcupine	Dumse

126

Portico	Pindhe
Portion	Baad, Hissa
Position	Aukat, Sthiti
Possess	Bhirnu
Possessed of capital	Mathwar
Possessed of power	Shaktishaale
Possibility	Sambhawataa,
	Sambhaawanaa
Possible	Sambhawa
Possibly	Sambhawataa
Postponed	Sthagit
Post-office	Hulakghar
Post	Padwe
Postman	Hulake
Postponement	Thate
Postulate	Swayamsiddha
Pot-bellied	Ghyampe
Potash	Potas
Potato	Aalu
Potbellied	Bhude
Potter	Kumhale
Poverty	Garebe, Daridrata
Powder	Bukune, Raina
Powdered	Churna
Power of thinking	Wicharshakti
Power	Ainch, Chakchake,
	Dabdaba,
	Samarthya
Powerful	Balwan
Practical	Prayogatmak
Practice	Abhyaas
Practised	Khalipa

Praise	Prashansa, Shyawase, Stuti, Syabase
Prattle	Phatphataunu
Prayer	Apel, Prarthana, Bandage, Binte
Precious	Jahade, Nagade
Precipice	Tarebher
Precipitous	Bhiralo
Predestination	Prarabdha
Prefix denoting own	Swa
Pregnancy	Garbha
Pregnant	Garbhine, Baljhanu
Preoccupation	Sura
Prepare	Parnu
Prepared in butter	Pakwanna
Prepared	Tatpar
Presence	Robakar, Haajire
Present	Upasthit, Kosele, Najrana, Pahur, Widyaman, Wirajman, Haajir
Preserve	Jogaunu
President	Sabhaapati
Press	Chapna, Pelna, Michna
Press down	Dabnu
Press hard	Khaadnu
Pressman	Samwaddata
Pressure of work	Taado, Lachharo
Pressure	Chaapaachaap, Dabau
Pretend	Topalnu
Pretension	Nihu

Prevailing	Prachalit
Prevention	Roka
Previous	Agillo
Price	Dam, Mulya
Pride of youth	Rupagarwa
Pride	Ahankar, Ghamand, Tujuk
Priest	Panda, Purohit
Primary	Prathamik, Prarambhik
Prime minister	Pradhanmantre, Mahamantre
Prince	Rajakumar, Shaha
Princely	Shahe
Princess	Rajakumare
Principal	Pradhan
Principal officer	Latha
Principal	Sau
Principle	Siddhanta
Print on cloth	Chhipnu
Print	Chhap
Printer	Mudraka
Printing-press	Chhapakhana, Pres
Printing	Mudran
Prison	Kaidkhana, Wandckhana
Prisoner	Kaide, Thunuwa, Wande
Prist	Pujahare, Brahman
Privacy	Ekanta
Privy	Charpe
Problem	Samasya

Procedure	Paddhati
Proceed	Janu
Procession	Julus
Proclamation	Chuinke
Procuress	Kutune
Produce of the land	Paidaware
Produced	Wyutpanna
Production	Samutpanna, Ubjane, Samutpati
Professional	Wyawasayik
Proficient	Nipun, Siddhahasta
Profit	Nafa, Munafa
Profligate	Luchcho
Progress	Unnati, Tarakke
Prohibition	Bingathyai
Prominent	Pramukha
Promise	Kabulnu, Prana, Bacha, Wachan, Wada
Promising	Honhar
Prone to mischief	Bigyaha
Pronoun	Sarwanama
Pronunciation	Uchcharan
Proof	Nissa, Praman, Buda, Sabuda
Prop	Tewa
Proper order	Thako
Proper	Uchit, Nyaye, Yukta, Yuktiyukta, Wajabe, Samuchit
Property	Jayajat, Jetha, Jhite
Proportionate division	Damasahe

130

Proposal	Prastawa
Prose	Gaddya
Prosecution	Pairawe
Prosperity	Phap, Samriddhi
Prosperous	Sampanna
Prostitute	Patar, Bhandine, Weshya
Prostrate	Ghopto, Lampasara
Protected	Sanrakchhit
Protection	Tran, Raksha, Sanrakchhyan
Proud of one's wealth	Dhanmatta
Proud	Uddhat, Ghamandi
Proved	Sabit
Provide	Jutaaunu
Providential	Bhagyashale
Provincial	Dehate
Provisions for a journey	Samala
Provocation	Chhedchhad, Sanko
Prowess	Karamat
Prying	Chiyo
Psychology	Manowigyan
Psychopathic	Matibhrashta
Public announcement	Ghoshna
Public information	Jahere
Public slander	Lokapawad
Public	Sarbajanik
Publication	Prakashan
Pudding fried in oil	Pakaude
Pudding	Payas
Puff of wind	Jhokka
Puff	Sarko

Pulse	Dal, Nade
Pump	Pamp
Pumpkin	Pharse
Punch	Mudke
Pungent	Tichchhar
Punishable	Dandaneya
Punishment	Danda, Sajaya
Pupil of the eye	Putale
Pupil	Shishya
Puppet	Kathputale
Purchase	Khared
Pure	Chokho, Thet, Shuddha
Purgative	Julaf
Purification	Sanskar
Purified	Sanskrit
Purity	Shuddhata
Purport	Marma
Purpose	Tatparya, Mansuwa
Pursue	Dapetnu
Pursuit	Dapeta, Lakheto
Pus	Pep
Push	Achetnu, Thelna. Dhakelnu, Paith
Put a few stitches in	Surkanu
Put on	Launu
Put to extreme pain	Pirolnu
Putrescent	Saduwa
Putting into force	Taamel
Putty	Puten
Puzzled	Ralla
Pyzama	Paijama
Quadrangular	Chaukune

Quadruped	Chaupaya
Quail	Battain
Quake	Kampa, Kamnu
Quality	Gun
Quarrel	Kalaha, Jhagada, Bajhabajh, Ladai
Quarrelling	Dagal-fasal
Quarrelsome	Kachingale, Kalyaha, Jhagadalu, Durmukha, Bajhuwa
Quarter part	Sawa
Quarterly	Traimasik
Quarters	Khalanga
Quartz	Pattharkoila, Manik
Queen consort	Patrane
Queen mother	Rajamata
Queen	Rane
Quest	Pahuna
Question and answer	Prashnottar
Question	Prashna, Sawala
Questionnaire	Prashnamaalaa
Quickly	Jhataajhat
Quiet	Shaanta
Quilt	Rajae, Sirak
Quilt pad	Dolaen
Quilted	Taguwa
Quince	Bihen
Quintessence	Nikhar
Quire of paper	Kore, Tau
Quite full	Bharpur
Quite thin and weak	Tasa

Quiver	Thokro
Quodibet	Sukshmaprashna
Quotation	Ukti
Quotient	Bhagfal
Repair	Marmmat
Religious act	Dharmakarma
Religious merit	Punya
Rough	Darun, Bidhange, Bodho, Michaahaa, Rukho
Round cushion	Chakte
Round shaped	Batulo, Pinda
Round	Gol, Dallo
Rounding	Kawa
Row	Pankti, Lahara, Hahu
Royal command	Hukum
Royal entrance	Raajadwaar
Royal family	Rajakula, Raajawansha
Royal insignia	Raajachinha
Royal mandate	Rajagyaa
Royal palace	Raajabhawan, Rajamahal
Royal physician	Rajabaidya
Royal place	Raajagriha, Rajadarbar
Royal priest	Gurujyu
Royal road	Raajapaatha, Raajamaarga
Royal throne	Raajagadde, Raajasinhaasana
Royal	Rajakeya
Royalist	Rajabhakta

Royalty	Raajabhakti
Rub	Raagadai, Malna, Ghasna
Rubbed	Maluwa
Rubber	Rawara
Rubbing oil on the body	Malish
Rubbish-hole	Rachhaana
Rude	Besomate
Rug	Raga
Ruin	Uchhitto, Nash
Ruined	Lethno, Widhwasta
Rule of three	Trairshik
Rule	Niyam, Rajai, Rula, Widhan
Ruminate	Ugraunu
Rumour	Sohora
Rump	Chaak
Run away	Bhagnu
Runner	Daudaha
Rupee	Taka, Rupiyaa
Rural song	Jhyaure
Rust	Khiya, Bakse
Rustice	Gawar
Rustling sound	Khasryankhusrun
Sack	Bhangro
Sacred-ashes	Bibhut, Wibhuta
Sacred-book	Shaastra
Sacred-grass	Dubo
Sacred-plant	Tulse
Sacred-cord	Janai
Sacrifice place	Yagyabhumi
Sacrificial vessel	Yagyapatra
Sacrifice	Hom-wali

Sacrificial Ministration	Yajamaane
Sacrificial ceremony	Yagyakarma
Sacrificial ladle	Suro
Sad	Udaas, Urath
Saddle-cloth	Jinpos
Saddle	Kathe
Sadness	Dikdare
Safe	Sef
Safety-pin	Kaata
Saffron	Keshar
Safron	Kumkum
Sailor	Jahaje
Saint	Rishi, Babaje, Mahatma, Muni, Siddha
Sal tree	Shala, Sakhuwa
Sal-ammoniac	Nausadar
Salary	Kista, Khanke, Tankhah
Sale	Bikre
Salesman	Bechaha
Saliva	Rala
Salt and acid	Nunchuk
Salt	Khar, Nimak, Nun
Saltless	Bilino, Alino
Salty	Khaarilo, Nunilo
Salutation	Dhog, Pranaam, Salaam
Salute	Salaame, Dhogna
Salvation	Parampad, Brahmagati, Moksha, Sadgati
Salvia	Thuk
Same as pahiro	Pairo

136

Same	Aijan
Sample	Namuna
Sanctioned in the sacred scriptures	Shastrokta
Sanctioned	Manjur
Sand	Paago, Baluwa
Sandal wood	Chandan, Shrekhanda
Sandals	Kharau
Sandy	Balauto
Sapling	Pothro
Sapphire	Ner
Saten	Satan
Satiated	Kritartha
Satiety	Mohoto
Satisfaction	Dhar, Rejha, Santosha
Satisfied	Kritakritya, Prasanna, Santushta
Saturday	Shaniwar
Sauce	Chhop, Tihun
Saucepan	Kadhaai
Saving	Bachat, Bachana
Savoury and keen	Tikkhar
Saw	Karaute
Saying	Bhannc
Scabbard	Dap
Scabies	Luto
Scale	Taraju
Scales of a fish	Katla
Scales	Tulo
Scandal	Kalanka
Scarcity	Kame

Scarf	Galebanda, Bhulayo
Scattered	Chhitar-bitar
Scented oil	Phulel
Scheme	Aayojanaa, Tarakeb, Yukti
Scholar	Widwan
School	Shikshalaya, Pathshala, Widyalaya, Skul
School bag	Basta
Science of spells	Mantrawidya
Science	Wigyaana
Scientific	Waigyaanika
Scissor	Sarauto
Scissors	Katarne, Kainche
Scoffer	Chose
Scoop	Panyu
Scorn	Gilla
Scorpion	Bichchhe
Scoundrel	Dushta
Scraggy	Haddetadde
Scrape off	Tachhnu
Screen	Pattal
Screwdriver	Pechkas, Martol
Script	Lipi
Scriptural	Waidika
Scripture	Dharmagrantha
Scuffle	Maramar
Sculptor	Aagre
Sculpture	Shilpakala
Scum	Gaaj
Scurf	Chaya
Sea-port	Bandargah

Sea	Samudra, Sagar
Seaerch	Chhanben
Seam	Siune
Search	Khoj, Talash
Season	Ritu
Seat of deer-skin	Mrigaasan
Seat	Aasan, Mudhaa, Sujane
Second-eldest son	Mahilo
Second-hand	Ardhano
Secret meaning	Mataka
Secret	Guhya, Ghuiro, Rahasya
Secretariat	Mantralaya
Section	Dafaa
Secure	Surakshit
Secured	Rakshita
Security	Dhito, Suraksha
Sediment	Ket, Thigrene, Nithar, Nithrene
Seed vessel	Bode
Seed	Geda, Dana, Bej, Beyaa
Seedless	Bedana
Seeds of cotton	Jyapu, Phuta
Seeds	Latte
Seizure by authority	Jafat
Select	Chunnu, Binna
Selection	Chhaatnu, Nirwachan
Self indulgent	Bhoko
Self-denying	Tyage
Self-government	Swaraajya
Self-willed	Manmoje

Self	Aafu, Nij
Selfish	Matlabe, Swaarthe
Selfishness	Swaartha
Sell	Bikauna, Bechna
Seller	Wikretaa
Selling	Wikraya
Send off	Bidai
Sensation	Sanasane
Senior	Bujruk
Sense	Chet, Mati,
	Suddhi, Hosh,
	Hoshhawas
Senseless	Achet
Sensual enjoyment	Wasana
Sensual	Lampata
Sentence	Wakya
Sentiment of sympathy	Karunras
Separate	Alag, Phutta,
	Begal
Separated	Wibhakta,
	Chhuttina, Wirahi
Separation	Wichchheda,
	Wiyoga
Series	Anukram, Dharr ,
	Silsila,
Serious calamity	Durghatnaa
Serious contemplation	Gaur
Serious quarrel	Dhusaakhaan
Serious	Gambher,
	Sthirchitta
Serpent	Sarpa
Servant	Kajiyan
Servant	Chakar, Nokar,
	Sewak

140

Service	Chakare, Nokare, Sewa
Sesamum seed	Til
Set apart	Chhutyaunu
Setting	Jadan
Settle	Basnu
Settled	Kayam, Thaparna
Settlement	Tungo
Seven and half	Sadhesat
Seven	Sat
Seventeen	Satra
Seventy	Sattare
Seventy-one	Ekhattar
Seventy-two	Bahattar
Seventy-three	Trihattar
Seventy-four	
Seventy five	Pachahattar
Seventy-six	Chhayahattar
Seventy-seven	Satahattar
Seventy-eight	Athhattar
Seventy-nine	Unase
Several	Anek
Several	Kaiyan, Dhum-chakra
Sewer	Dhal
Sewing	Silaai
Sexual enjoyment	Rasaranga
Sexual intercourse	Ratidan, Sahawaas
Shackles	Thingura
Shaddock	Jyamer, Bhogate
Shade	Ojhel, Chhahare
Shadow	Sep
Shady	Sepilo
Shake	Hallana

141

Shake off	Jharnu
Shake up	Mathnu
Shaking	Hilai
Shame-faced	Lajalu
Shame	Lajja, Sharama
Shameless (female)	Satarne
Shameless	Nakachcharo, Nirlajja, Besharam, Lawastaro
Shape and appearance	Chhaat-kaat
Shape	Anuhaar, Akar, Swarup
Shapeless stick	Lathingare
Shapeless	Bedaul
Share	Bhaag
Sharing	Baadchund
Sharp wit	Sukshmabuddhi
Sharp-eyed	Sukshmadarshi
Sharp	Tekho, Pero
Sharped	Dharilo
Sharpening	Shan
Shaving	Hajamat
Shawl	Khasto, Dupatta, Dosalla
Shed	Katero
Sheet	Chaddar, Pachheura
She goat	Baakhre
Shelf	Takhta
Shelter	Aasaraa, Ot, Sharana, Sahyaala
Shelterless	Nirashrya
Shepherd	Gothalo

Shield	Dhal
Shin	Nalehad
Shining	Jhakajhak,
	Jhalmalla,
	Dedepyaman
Ship	Jahaj
Shirt	Kamej
Shiver with cold	Thartharaunu
Shoe sole	Taluwa
Shoe-maker	Chamaar, Sarke
Shoes	Juttaa
Shop	Dokaan, Pasal
Shopkeeper	Bajaariyaa,
	Dokandar
Short-cut	Chhekaro
Short-necked	Nyachche
Short	Chhoto, Bhudulke
Shortstatured	Ganto
Shoulder	Kaadh, Kum
Shout	Karaunu
Shove	Dhakka
Show	Thassaa, Dekhau,
	Bhadak
Showers	Jhare
Showy	Dekhauwa,
	Bhadkilo,
	Bharkanu
Shrike	Bahunechare
Shrill (of voice)	Surilo
Shrimp	Jhenge
Shrink	Pasaaginu
Shroud	Katro
Shrunk	Sankuchit
Shy	Lajjalu

143

Sick-bed	Thala
Sick	Birame, Roge
Sicked	Pathara
Sickle	Khurpa, Hasiyaa
Side	Paksha
Sieve	Chalne
Sigh	Suskeraa
Sight-seer	Tamashe
Sight	Drishya
Sign of sex	Linga
Sign	Chinha
Signal	Ishara
Signature	Dastakhat, Hastakchhar
Significance	Mahattwa
Signs of the Zodiac	Rashi
Silence	Chup
Silk-cotton-tree	Simal
Silk	Resham
Silken cloth	Muga
Silkworm	Reshama-kera
Silky	Reshame, Wiwekahen, Sille
Silver age	Treta
Silver	Chaade
Similar	Saddasha
Similarity	Samanta
Simple	Winet, Bholabhala, Sada, Sudho
Simpleton	Latosojho
Simplicity	Saralata
Sing	Gaunu
Singer	Gawaiya

Singing	Alaap
Single life	Brahmacharya
Single	Ekohoro
Sinner	Widharme
Sister-in-law	Sale
Situated	Sthit
Situation	Hal
Six	Chha
Sixteen	Sorha
Sixty-one	Eksatthe
Sixty-two	Bayasatthe
Sixty-three	Trisatthe
Sixty-four	Chausatthe
Sixty-five	Painsatthe
Sixty-six	Chhayasatthe
Sixty-seven	Satsatthe
Sixty-eight	Athsatthe
Sixty-nine	Unahattar
Sixty	Sathe
Size and stature	Deldaul
Size	Kad
Skeleton	Kankal
Skilful	Pokhta
Skill	Kaushal, Sepa
Skin of tree	Chhala
Skin	Khal
Skinflint	Makkhechus
Skirt	Phariya, Gunyu, Lahanga, Sare
Sky	Aakaash, Megha-mandal, Sagar
Slacker	Lose
Slander	Chukli, Durwachan

Slanting	Terso
Slap	Chadkan, Dhussa, Labata
Slapping	Thappad
Slate for roofing	Jhingate
Slaughter	Katakat
Slave	Kariya
Slavery	Gulame
Sleep	Nidra
Sleeve of a garment	Mohoto
Sleeve	Bahulo
Slight repair	Taltul
Slim	Patale
Slime	Hilo
Slip-knot	Surkaune
Slippery	Chiplo
Slipping away	Swatta
Slough of a snake	Kaachule
Slow	Dhema, Luse
Small basket	Kadale
Small box	Batta
Small boy	Balak, Bhura
Small bridge	Phatke
Small bundle	Gathare
Small bush	Jhar
Small cardamom	Sukumel
Small Copper Jar	Hatar
Small cup-shaped cymbals	Majura
Small flame	Dhipko
Small girl	Bhure
Small hole	Khope
Small hut	Khopro
Small Jar	Bhudulko
Small pack	Toshdaan

146

Small part	Lesha
Small piece	Tyandro, Kudkaa
Small pitcher	Gagre
Small purse	Thaile
Small rivulet	Naalaa
Small swelling	Dabar
Small-minded	Kchhyudra
Small-pox	Bifar, Shetala
Small	Ope, Jheno
Smart	Chankha, Jhankanu, Thamthamaudo
Smashed	Kichmich
Smile	Muskan
Smiling	Hasilo
Smithy	Jyasa
Smoke-coloured	Dhusro
Smoke	Dhuaa
Smoker	Nashabaj
Smooth and round	Dolo
Smooth	Salakka
Snail	Chiplekero
Snake-gourd	Chichindo
Snake	Nag, Sulsule
Snare	Dharap, Phanda
Snarp-tongued	Duchchhar
Snatch away	Thutnu
Sneakingly	Sutukka
Sneeze	Chhink, Chhyu, Hachchhiu
Snout	Thutuno
Snow mountain	Himaal
Snow-clad mountain	Himgiri
Snow	Hiu, Him

147

Snuff	Nas
So great	Utro
So much	Tyattiko, Yatti
Soap-nut	Rittho
Soap	Sabun
Sobbing	Sukkasukka
Social behaviour	Lokachara
Social service	Lokasewa
Social	Samajik
Socialism	Saamyawaad
Socialistic	Saamyawaade
Society	Samaja
Socket of the eye	Gaha
Socks	Mojaa
Soda water	Sodapane
Soda	Soda
Soft pith of a cucumber etc	Gidro
Soft wool	Pasham
Soft woollen cloth	Maleda
Soft	Kamalo, Kalilo, Naram, Mihe, Mridu
Softness	Mridutaa
Solace	Dilasa
Solar eclipse	Suryagrahana
Soldier	Tilingo, Sipahe, Sainik
Sole of shoe	Paitalo
Solicitation	Yachana
Solid	Khadilo
Solution	Samadhan
Some	Alikataa, Kunai, Kehe
Somehow or other	Kaso-kaso

148

Someone	Phalano
Sometimes	Kahilekahen
Somewhat	Rate
Somewhere	Ktai, Kahen
Son-in-law	Juwain
Son	Chhoro, Putra, Suta
Song	Rasiya, Gana, Get, Gelo, Raga
Song of praise	Bhajan
Soon	Chaado
Sophistry	Mithyawad
Sorceror	Bhedaha
Sorcery	Yantramantra
Sorrow	Gunaso, Bismat, Wishada
Sorrowful	Udase
Soul	Chaitanya
Sound of footstep	Aahat
Sound-winded	Dam-pach
Sound	Aawaaj
Soundly	Nirghat
Soup	Suruwa
Sour	Amilo, Saadhnu
Source	Jaro, Nikas, Mul
Sourcerer	Dhame
Southern	Dakshini
Sovereignty	Sarbabhaumikata
Sow	Bhune
Soyabean	Bhatmas
Spade	Kodale
Spades (in cards)	Suratha
Spare time	Phursat
Sparrow	Bhangero

Speak carelessly	Bhatbhataunu
Speak loudly in pride	Dukranu
Speaker	Wakta,
	Sabhamukha
Special oblation to God	Naibedya
Special	Khas, Wishesha
Specialist	Wisheshagyaa
Speciality	Wisheshataa
Specification	Kitan
Specimen	Pharma
Speck or drop	Thopo
Spectacles	Chashma
Spectacle	Ramita
Spectator	Darshak
Speech and promise	Bolkabol
Speech	Bat, Bhashan,
	Waktabya, Wacha
Spelling	Hijje
Spendthrift	Dhanfukuwa
Spices	Marmasala
Spider	Makuro
Spinach	Palungo
Spin	Katna
Spinning-wheel	Charkha
Spirit	Pret, Tejab, Sato
Spiritual teacher	Rajaguru
Spiritual	Aadhyaatmik
Spittle	Phik
Spittoon	Thukdane,
	Phikdaan
Spleen	Phiyo
Splendid	Jhillimile
Splinter	Chhesko
Split cane	Choyo

Split wood	Kaptero
Split	Udhrana
Spoilage	Lataluta
Spoilt	Dushit, Khaharina
Sponging son in law	Ghar-Jwaain
Sponge-gourd	Ghiraula
Sponger	Bhatuwa
Spoon	Chamchaa
Sporadic	Phaatphute
Sport	Kreda
Spotted deer	Chittal
Spoted	Thople
Spotted	Jhalemale
Spray of water	Phuhara
Spread here and there	Pasaro, Machchaunu
Spread over	Lasarnu
Spreading	Phailawat, Saruwa
Sprightly	Phurtiwal
Spring	Jhamat, Bahar
Sprout	Ankur, Pasaunu
Spy	Chewa
Squint-eyed	Dero
Squirrel	Lokharke
Stable	Tabela
Stack of hay	Kuniyo
Stag	Jhaak
Stagecraft	Natyakala
Stain	Dag, Lanchhana
Stair-case	Bharyan
Stale	Base
Stalk	Daath
Stammerer	Bhakbhake
Stamp	Bajarnu, Mudra

Standard-bearer	Jhande, Nishaan
Standing alone	Thingo
Standing dive	Budulke
Standing	Khadaa
Stanza	Shloka
Star	Taaraa
Starch	Kae
Startled	Khangranga
State Prince	Rajauto
State of hesitation	Dodhar
State service	Jager
Statement	Bakpatra, Kaifiyat, Bachan, Bhanai
Statesmanship	Rajanetigyata
Steadiness	Wichalle
Steady	Darbilo
Steamer	Agnibot
Steel	Ispat
Steep	Karaalo
Steeple	Gajur
Stem of sugarcane	Laakro
Step mother	Wimatri
Step-son	Jhadkelo
Step	Kadam, Khutkela, Deg, Phatko
Stick	Chhade, Lahuro, Lathe
Stickiness	Lassa
Sticky	Chyat-chyat, Lassadara, Lesailo
Stiff and cold	Thandaram
Stiff fruit-juice jelly	Maadaa
Stiff	Tharro
Stiletto	Soilo

152

Stimulation	Uttejanaa
Sting of a hornet	Khel
Stinging	Marmabhede
Stirrup	Rikaba
Stitch	Taaka
Stockings	Juraf
Stomach	Pet
Stomach	Bhude, Ladro
Stone or kerne	Koya
Stone plate	Patthare
Stone-hearted	Nirdaye
Stone	Dhungo, Patthar, Shila
Stony	Pattharilo
Stool	Jhada
Stooling	Hagai
Stop	Thamna, Rokna
Stopped	Banda
Store-house	Dhukute, Bhandar
Store-keeper	Bhandaare
Store	Khajaanaa, Godaam
Storey	Tala
Story	Kathaa, Kahane, Kissa
Stove	Tawa
Strange	Anauthaa, Parchakre, Wichitra
Strangeness	Wichitrataa
Straw	Paral
Stray cases	Biralakote
Steal	Chorna
Stream of milk	Sirko

153

Stream of water	Bhangalo
Streaming	Pharpharahat, Balindra
Strength of hands	Bahubal
Strength	Werya, Shakti
Strenuous	Yatnawan
Strict	Kharo
Strictness	Kadai
Strike	Hartal
Striking	Hanai
Stormwind	Aadhe
Strong-minded	Manaswe
Strong	Jabbar, Prabal , Majbut
Structure	Banawat
Struggle	Tana-tan, Marpet
Stubble	Buchko
Stubborn	Jiraha
Stubborness	Lindhedhipe
Studied	Jadau
Student	Chelo, Widyarthe, Shiksharthe
Study	Adhyayan, Pathan, Padhai
Stumbling	Thes
Stump	Thuto
Stupid	Abujh, Nadan, Nasamajh, Mudha, Lathuwa, Hussu
Style and titles	Prashasti
Style	Shaile
Stylish fashion	Dhaacha
Sub story	Upakatha
Sub-branch	Binga

Subject matter	Bhawartha
Subject	Prasanga, Raite
Subjugation	Daman
Subjunctive (gram)	Wisheshya
Subscriber	Dane
Subsistence of a year	Warshashana
Substance	Sar, Sarans
Substitute	Bapat, Sato
Subtle	Sukshma
Subtlety	Sukshmataa
Suburb	Kaath
Success	Safalataa, Safalaya, Siddhi
Successful	Safala
Suck	Chusnu
Suckling	Dudhe
Sudden collision	Jamkaabhet
Suddenly	Akasmaat, Ekdam, Ekkaasi, Syatta
Suffering	Peda, Wyatha
Sufficiency	Chhelokhclo
Sufficient riches	Auladaula
Sufficient	Purna
Suffix in grammar	Pratyaya
Suffix	Purwak
Suffocation	Usin-pasin
Sugar	Chine
Sugarcandy	Mishre
Sugarcane	Ukhu
Suicide	Apahattyaa
Suitable	Upayoge, Mutawika, Yogya
Sulphate of iron	Herakase
Sulphur	Gandhak

155

Summer season	Garme
Summer	Greshma
Summit	Takuro
Sun flower	Suryamukhe
Sun	Surya
Sunlight	Pahaar
Sunny	Pahaarilo
Sunshine	Gham
Superior	Nek, Wishishta, Shreshtha
Superiority	Pradhanta, Wishishtata, Shreshthata
Supervision	Dekhrekh, Nigrane, Nirekshan, Herwichar
Supervisor	Adhyakchhya, Nirekshak
Suppliant	Prarthe
Support	Aadhaar, Bhar, Samarthan, Sahara
Supporter	Annadaataa, Patron, Samarthaka
Suppress	Thichnu
Supreme spirit	Parmatma
Supreme	Parameshwar, Sarwashreshtha
Surety for good conduct	Phel-jamane
Surety	Jamane
Surface	Tah
Surplus	Ubro

Surprise	Aashcharya, Wismaya
Surprise inspection	Chhadke
Surprised	Jilla, Ranabhulla, Wismita
Surrender	Samarpana
Surroundings	Serofero
Survey	Naape
Surveying	Paimaish
Surveyor	Dangol
Suspend	Jhundyaunu
Suspicious	Bhramatmak
Swallow	Gauthale
Swampy land	Thalthale
Swan	Panehaas
Sweat	Pasina
Sweepings	Jhadubadharu
Sweet and sarow	Katmiro
Sweet cake	Malpuwa
Sweet meat	Manbhog, Rasagulla
Sweet-seller	Halwai
Sweet smell	Magmag, Mahak, Sugandha
Sweet taste	Guliyo
Sweet will	Manpare
Sweet-potato	Shakkharkhanda
Sweet	Madhur, Metho, Rochaka
Sweetness	Madhurtaa, Madhurya, Mithaas
Sweets	Mithaai
Swimming	Paude

Swing	Jhulana, Pen
Sword	Kirech, Khadga
Sycophant	Khushaamade
Syllabus	Pathyakram
Symbol	Sanketa
Sympathy	Sahaanubhuti
Synthetic	Sanyogik
Syphilis	Bhiringe
Syringe	Pachka
Syrup	Sarwat
Systematically	Yathakrama
Tabernacle	Pujakotha
Table of contents	Dehaya, Phirista
Tack	Phulkela
Tail	Puchchhar
Tailless	Lindo
Tailor-bird	Phisto
Tailor	Darje
Take fright	Tarsanu
Take hold of	Pakadnu, Samatnu
Take to task	Sepnu
Taking by force	Luchhachude
Taking rest	Lethana
Talcom powder	Pha
Talk	Bolnu
Talk nonsense	Baknu
Talkative	Kuraute, Nakhramaaulo, Bakbake
Talkativeness	Nakhramaaulyain
Tall and thin	Tingro
Tall	Dhabbu, Dhere
Tamarind fruit	Amile
Tambourine	Khainjade, Damfu

158

Tangled hair	Jagalto
Tank	Kunda
Tape	Sanjapa
Target	Taro, Nishaanaa
Tassel	Ijar, Phurko
Taste	Chakhnu, Swad
Tasteless	Khallo, Tarro, Niras, Phikka
Tasting	Swaadishta
Tasty	Swaadilo
Taunt	Chhednu
Tax	Kar, Nal, Mahasul
Taxes paid to a king	Rajakar
Tea	Chiya
Teacher	Adhyapak, Guru, Shikshaka
Teaching of the Vedas	Brahmawad
Teaching	Upadesh, Shikshana
Teak tree	Sajiwana
Tear down	Lachnu
Tear with teeth	Luchhnu
Tear	Aasu
Tearing	Widaraka
Tears	Netrajal
Tease	Jiskyaunu
Talent	Yogyataa
Telescope	Durben
Tell-tale	Polaha
Tempest	Hurc
Temple	Kanchat, Dewal, Kansire, Mandir
Temporary	Kchhyanik
Temprature	Tapman

159

Temptation	Bahakaw
Ten per cent	Dashaud
Ten sheets of paper	Dhep
Ten	Dash
Tenant-farmer	Mohe
Tent pitcher	Pipa
Tent	Tumbo, Pal
Tenth	Dashau
Termite	Dhamiro
Terrace	Kause
Terrible fight	Ghamasan
Terrible	Aghor, Ugra, Karaal, Ghor, Bhyankar, Bhem, Bheshma
Test	Jaach
Tether	Pagaha
Than	Bhanda
Thanks	Dhanyawad
That much	Tyati
That same	Uhe, Tyae
That side	Tyata
That	So
Thatch	Khar
The Hades	Nagalok
The abode of Brahma	Satyaloka
The abode of Death	Yamapure
The abode of Vishnu	Waikuntha
The abode of the blessed	Punyalok
The acquirement of pleasure	Bhoglabh
The act of boring	Bhedan
The act of sleeping	Sukala
The act of sprinkling	Chhyapai
The act of supporting	Lole

The aloes plant	Elwa
The appearance	Sakala
The bright half of the lunar month	Shuklapaksha
The citron-leaved fig tree	Pakhare
The coming third year	Paraghau
The commencing of reading & writing	Widyarambha
The completion of fruits	Lataramma
The confluence of three rivers	Triwene
The confluence of two rivers	Dobhan
The coral tree	Parijat
The dahlia	Lahaure
The dark fortnight of Aswin	Pitripaksha
The dark half of a month	Purpaksha
The dative case (gram)	Sampradana
The day after tomorrow	Parse
The day of the new moon	Ause
The deodar-tree	Dewadaru
The descending node of the moon	Ketu
The digestive organs	Paksathale
The disease of mumps	Haade
The end of the year	Saltamam
The festival of triumph	Wijayotsawa
The first day of a month	Sankranti
The five sense organs	Panchakarmen-driya
The foot of a mountain	Phede
The forehead	Lalata
The fork made by two pieces of wood	Choke
The game of hide-and-seek	Kanekanepichcl
The holt fig tree	Pippal

161

The husk of lentils	Kunauro
The internal pain	Markaa
The intoxicating hemp	Bhan
The king-crow	Chibhe
The knowledge of self	Mahagyan
The last gasp	Hikihiki
The last year	Pohor
The light fortnight of a lunar month	Sude
The lobe of the ear	Lote
The manner of carrying	Bokai
The maternal home of a woman	Maait
The means of support	Nirwaha
The menses	Rajodharma
The navel	Naito, Nabhe
The nettle	Sisnu
The noose of death	Kalpash, Mahapash
The ocean	Nadekant
The other side	Par
The other world	Paratra
The pangs of death	Yamayatana
The part of a city	Mahalla
The parting in the hair	Siudo
The paternal home of daughter	Maite
The planet Neptune	Rahu
The planet Saturn	Shani
The planet Venus	Shukra
The plant Annsleia spinosa	Makhaanaa
The plant	Bakainu
The polar region	Dhruwalok
The present time	Wartamana
The quality of passion	Rajoguna

The records of a case	Misil
The rope of leaves	Lokato
The ruddy goose	Chakhewa
The ruins of buildings	Bhagnaawa-shesh
The sago	Sabudana
The same	Sohe
The second day of a lunar fortnight	Dwateya
The secretion of the eyes	Chipraa
The seventh day of a lunar fortnight	Saptame
The sides	Kolte
The sixth day of a lunar month	Shashthe
The snipe	Chaha
The span of hand	Bitta
The strength of wisdom	Buddhibal
The string used for revolving a churn	Nete
The suburb of a town	Mofasal
The tenh day of a lunar fortnight	Dashme
The tenth day of bright half of jestha	Dashahara
The three myrobalans	Trifala
The tip of a needle	Nathre
The top of head	Purpuro
The tree Butea frondosa	Palas
The tree Symplocos race-moze	Lodha
The tree 'Aegle marmelos'	Bel
The twelfth day of a lunar fortnight	Dwadashe
The upper jaw	Chyapu

163

The vital spot	Matak
The wheel of time	Kalchakra
The whole body	Sarwanga
The work of buying and selling	Bechbikhan
The work of daubing	Lipadhasa
The world of men	Martyalok
The year before last	Parar
Theatre	Natyashala, Rangashala
Theft	Chore
Then	Uhile, Taba
Theoretical	Saiddhantik
There	Uhaa, Wahaa
Thereafter	Upranta
Therefore	Tasartha
Thermometer	Digre
They	Te
Thick though flat	Dhose
Thick	Ghana, Baklo , Mota
Thicket	Jhade
Thickness	Motai
Thief	Chor
Thigh	Jaagh, Tighro
Thimble	Autarnu
Thin as water	Panyalo
Thin strip	Pata
Thin	Patala, Mihen, Sepro
Thing	Chej, Thok, Padartha, Paasula, Mal, Wastu
Think of	Kalpanu, Taknu
Think over	Lakhnu

Thinker	Wichare
Third-eldest	Saahilo
Third	Tesro
Thirst	Tirkha, Tirsana, Dhet, Pyas
Thirsty	Pyase
Thirteen	Tera
Thirteenth lunar day	Trayodashe
Thirteenth	Terau
Thirty	Tes
Thirty-one	Ektes
Thirty-two	Battes
Thirty three	Tetes
Thirty-four	Chautes
Thirty-five	Paintes
Thirty-six	Chhattes
Thirty seven	Sattes
Thirty-eight	Athtes
Thirty-nine	Unanchales
This world	Ihalok
This	Yo
Thorn	Kaadho
Thou	Ta
Thought	Manas, Lakha
Thoughtful	Dhyane, Wicharwan
Thousand	Hajar
Thread	Dhago
Threat	Tokso, Dhamke, Haak
Three quarters	Paune
Three times	Tiguna, Trikal
Three	Ten
Threshing-floo	Khalo

Thresing	Dain
Thrice	Tebbar
Throat	Kantha
Throat	Gala, Ghaate, Ghokro
Throne	Sinhasan
Through and through	Nithrukka
Through	Marfat
Throw	Phyaaknu, Milkaunu
Thumb (of hand)	Budheaulo
Thumb	Autho
Thunder-bolt	Wajra, Wajrapata
Thursday	Brihaspati
Ticklishness	Kutkute
Tie	Paso
Tiger's skin	Baghambaru
Tiger	Bagh
Tight	Sankerna
Tigress	Baghine
Till	Paryanta, Samma
Timbal	Nagara
Timber	Timba
Time server	Tapartuyyaa
Time-serving	Paripath
Time	Kal, Jamana, Pal Pher, Bakhat, Ba Yama, Wela, Samaya
Timid	Katar
Tin-box	Dhwan
Tinkling	Jhankar
Tiny	Sano
Tip	Chuchcho

166

Tired	Thakit
Tithe	Bethe
Title	Upadhi, Shirshaka
Tittle-tattle	Gaf
To abort	Tuhaunu
To ache rheumatism	Makmakaunu
To act over boldly	Hepnu
To add	Thapnu
To aim at	Dagnu
To allow to be swollen	Dhadyaunu
To allure	Lalachaunu
To appear to be	Bhasnu
To appease	Manaunu
To appoint	Khataunu
To assemble	Bathannu
To avoid decency	Pattinu
To awake	Jagaunu, Bauranu
To bark	Bhuknu
To be agitated	Talbalaunu
To be appreciated	Jachnu
To be at a loss	Tolaunu
To be auspicious	Phapnu
To be bent by age	Khunrinu
To be benumbed	Kathinu
To be bewildered	Haskanu
To be bundled up	Gutmutinu
To be clouded	Rudinu
To be compelled	Natthinu
To be conceited	Timkinu
To be concluded	Tunginu
To be confined to bed	Thachchinu
To be crestfallen	Lutrinu
To be cross	Jhokinu
To be crushed	Kuchchinu

167

To be damp	Osinu
To be dazzled	Tirmiraunu
To be deceived	Chhakinu
To be dilatory	Nichhaunu
To be discouraged	Ochhaunu, Lotinu
To be diseased	Rogaunu
To be doubtful	Bharmanaunu
To be dragged	Ghisranu
To be drawn	Ghissinu
To be dried up	Rukhinu
To be dumb	Latinu
To be eager	Tarkharaunu
To be elongated	Lamminu
To be emboldened	Hausinu
To be empty	Taktakinu
To be evasive	Phisolnu
To be fanned	Hamkanu
To be fashionably dressed	Thaatinu
To be finished eating	Butyainu
To be finished	Sakinu
To be flattened	Cheptinu, Phurphurinu
To be foolish	Hussinu
To be ill for long	Thalinu
To be in a hurry	Chatpataunu, Hadbadaunu, Hatpataunu
To be in coils	Gudlinu
To be intoxicated	Latthinu
To be irritated	Chidhinu
To be kept on one side	Thankinu
To be knocked	Takkaraunu
To be late	Pachhaunu
To be liked	Ruchnu

To be loaded with works	Ladinu
To be loosened	Khuskanu
To be lowered	Hochinu
To be mistaken	Jhukkinu
To be on pins and needles	Tulbulaunu
To be partly	Dagalchinu
To be perfumed	Mahakaunu
To be piled	Thuprinu
To be pleased	Ramnu
To be pressed down	Thichinu
To be prosperous	Sablaunu
To be prostrate	Tersinu
To be pure	Sanlanu
To be raised	Uksanu
To be remove	Bhutlinu
To be repeated	Doharinu
To be seen	Herinu
To be sharpened	Tikharinu
To be shut up	Thuninu
To be smudged	Latapatinu
To be solved satisfactorily	Patnu
To be sourtempered	Tathmaraunu
To be startled	Jhaskanu
To be tempted	Lobhinu
To be thin	Seprinu
To be thread	Unnu
To be tightened well	Maskanu
To be torn	Dhaskanu
To be tossed up	Urlanu
To be twisted	Markanu,
	Latharinu, Ludinu
To be underbaked	Jhilsinu
To be united	Joltinu,
	Lathangrinu

169

To be upset	Ghoptinu
To beat bitterly	Chutnu
To become giddy	Rennu
To become narrow	Saaghurinu
To become sterile	Bailhinu
To become unmanly	Lotrinu
To become wrinkled	Chaurinu
To beg for help	Guharnu
To beg	Magnu
To beget	Janmaunu
To begin	Thalnu
To behave indecorously	Ullinu
To bend over	Markaunu
To bite	Dasnu
To brand	Damnu
To break in animals	Daunu
To break through	Bhednu
To break	Phutaunu,
	Bhaachnu
To breathe hard	Dhakaunu
To bring down	Oralnu
To bring up	Hurkaunu
To bury	Gadnu
To buy	Kinnu, Besaunu
To call loudly	Haparnu
To call	Daknu, Bolaunu,
	Haaknu
To card cotton	Uitnu
To carry	Boknu
To carve	Kudnu
To catch hold of	Samaunu
To catch	Athyaunu
To cause to be damped	Osaunu
To cause to be filled	Bharaunu

To cause to be given	Dilaunu
To cause to be put in writing	Daraunu
To cause to be read	Padhaunu
To cause to be tested	Chakhaunu
To cause to bend	Nuhaunu
To cause to caress	Ladinu
To cause to drink	Pilaunu
To cause to drop	Khasalnu
To cause to fight	Judhaunu
To cause to flourish	Saparnu
To cause to flow	Bagaunu
To cause to grow	Umarnu
To cause to rot	Kuhaunu
To cause to run away	Bhagaunu, Suinkyaunu
To cause to sit down	Baithyaunu
To cause to sleep	Sutaunu
To cause to sound	Bajaunu
To cause to stir wind	Batasinu
To cause to stool	Hagaunu
To cause to walk	Hindaunu
To cause to wither	Oilyaunu
To challenge	Lalakarnu
To change	Phernu
To chase	Lakhetnu
To chastise	Jhaatnu
To cheat by flattery	Daasnu, Dangyaunu
To cheat	Chhalnu
To chew susurringly	Marmaryaunu
To choose	Chhannu, Rojnu
To clean out	Ugalnu
To cleanse with ashes	Ultanu

171

To cleanse	Khakalnu, Nikharnu
To clear (forest)	Ujarnu
To clear the throat	Khakarnu
To come between	Chheknu
To come loose	Phuklanu
To come quite close	Dhepnu
To come to perfection	Chhippinu
To commit a mistake	Biraunu
To compare	Daajnu, Bhidaunu
To compel	Natthyaunu
To conceive	Gadhnu, Dhussinu
To constantly remind	Thosnu
To contaminate	Bhornu
To coo	Ghurnu
To cook by boiling	Usinnu
To copy	Sarnu
To cough	Khoknu, Odhnu, Chhaunu, Dhaknu
To crack	Charkanu, Phutnu
To crawl	Ghasranu
To crowd round	Jhumminu
To cry out loudly	Kurlanu
To curl up	Ghugurinu
To curse	Dhikkarnu
To cut a sorry figure	Nichchinu
To cut a throat	Retnu
To cut	Katnu, Phaadnu
To dangle	Jhulkyaunu
To dare	Surinu
To deceive	Jhukkyaunu, Thagnu
To decide	Chhinnu
To defecate	Gobryaunu

172

To demolish	Bhaskaunu
To deprive of clothes	Nangyaunu
To descend	Orlanu, Utranu, Bhasinu
To develop	Phashtaunu
To dig into	Khodalnu
To dig up	Udhinnu
To dilate	Phulnu
To dissolve	Phetnu, Bilaunu, Hudalnu
To distil	Nithranu
To disturb	Kalbalyaunu
To disunite	Phataunu
To do away with	Masnu
To do one's best	Nethnu
To dote	Pulpulyaunu
To drag along by force	Lachharnu
To drag	Ghisarnu
To draw	Khinchnu, Tannu
To drink	Piunu
To drip	Tapkanu
To drive out	Dhapaunu
To drive	Khednu
To dry	Gumsinu, Sukaunu
To dust	Taktakyaunu
To eject saliva	Thuknu
To emerge	Niklanu
To enchant	Mantranu
To entice	Phuslyaunu
To entrap	Phasaunu
To entrust	Sumpanu
To erect	Thadyaunu
To escape	Umkanu, Suinkinu
To evade	Tarnu

173

To exchange rupees, notes, etc	Bhajaunu
To exchange	Satnu
To excite	Ubhadnu
To extend	Lamchyaunu
To extinguish	Nibhnu
To extort by trickery	Dhutnu
To fade	Oilaunu
To fall heavily	Bajranu
To fall in a large quantity	Oirinu
To fall in little drops	Taptapaunu
To fall in love	Lahasinu
To fall into a drowse	Lolinu
To fall off	Jharnu
To fall	Khasnu, Girnu, Dabnu
To fan	Hamkaunu
To fancy	Kathnu
To fart	Padnu
To feed	Palnu
To feel a burning sensation	Jhamjhamaunu
To feel acute pain	Katkatinu, Chaskanu
To feel drowsy or sleepy	Lolaunu
To feel hot and tired	Dhapinu
To feel weary	Thaknu
To feel	Chhamnu
To fight	Ladnu
To file	Retnu, Sernu
To fill	Bharnu
To finish eating	Butyaunu
To finish or do once	Ekohoryaunu
To fix	Theknu
To flame	Raakkinu

174

To flare up	Tamtamaunu, Dankanu
To flash	Chadkanu
To flater	Phatphataunu
To flatter	Phurphuryaunu
To flutter	Phurnu
To flinch	Ghaskanu
To fling	Huttyaunu
To flock together	Dhuirinu
To flourish	Maulaunu, Sapranu
To flow	Ragnu
To flower	Phakranu
To fold	Patyaunu
To foment	Sekaunu
To forget	Birsaunu
To form holes in	Chhednu
To freeze	Jamnu
To frequent	Dhaunu
To frighten away	Dachkaunu
To fry in oil or ghee	Jhannu
To fry	Bhutnu
To gallop	Kudaunu
To get angry	Phankanu, Risaunu
To get heated	Rapinu, Phasnu
To get leisure	Phuskanu
To get loose	Phutkanu
To get permission	Baksaunu
To get plucked	Gultinu
To get tired	Pattaunu
To get wet	Bhijnu, Rujhnu
To get	Paunu
To give a sounding slap	Dhukdhukyaunu

175

To give one seizing from another	Mosnu
To give reluctantly	Taskyaunu
To give rest	Bisaunu
To give the lie to	Labarnu
To go down	Pachharinu
To go free	Phuknu
To go from one place to another	Sarnu
To go in	Pasnu, Bhitrinu
To go mad	Sankanu
To graze	Charaunu, Charnu
To grind	Pindhnu
To grope	Tatolnu
To grow bushy	Jhaaginu
To grow cool	Chisinu
To grow fat	Motaunu, Suinthaunu
To grow furious	Sangralinu
To grow hard	Jarkharinu, Jarrinu
To grow tight	Tankanu
To grow	Ubjanu
To grumble	Gungunaunu
To guess	Tadnu
To gulp	Kaplyaunu
To hang about	Rallinu
To hang	Latkaunu, Larkanu
To harass	Sataunu
To harp on same string	Thunnu
To hatch eggs	Othranu
To have carried	Bokaunu
To have hiccough	Hiknu
To heap	Thuparnu
To help	Saghaunu

176

To hesitate	Ankanaunu
To hitch	Hichkichaunu
To hoard	Kumlyaunu
To hold open	Thapnu
To hook up	Huchchyaunu
To hum	Bhanbhanaunu, Hunhunaunu
To hurl	Hurrryaunu
To inflame	Poinu
To inflate	Phulaunu
To irritate	Saksakaunu
To itch	Chilaunu
To jeer at	Gijyaunu
To join	Gaasnu, Gabhnu
To jump	Ufranu, Phatkanu
To keep guard	Kurnhu
To keep waiting	Kuraunu
To kick spurn tread	Lattyaunu
To kick	Thukryaunu
To kindle	Salkanu
To knock down	Bhatkaunu
To knock	Khatkhataunu
To knowk	Ghachghachyaunu
To last	Tiknu, Thegnu
To laugh at	Khijyaunu
To leap over	Phaadnu
To leave	Chhodnu
To let cool after cooking	Othaunu
To let in	Siuranu
To lick	Chatnu, Lapkaunu
To lie down carelessly	Pasarinu
To lie in wait	Dhknu
To lie motionless	Kuchrinu
To lie	Dhaatnu

177

To lift	Ujaunu
To like	Ruchaunu
To load	Ladnu
To loaf	Rangelinu
To look after	Sahyarnu
To look as if concealing	Dapkanu
To look minutely	Niyalnu
To look yellowish	Pahenlinu
To loose	Gumaunu, Phunu
To lose appetite	Mohatinu
To lose greasiness	Phusrinu
To lose	Haraunu, Harnu
To lower	Hochyaunu
To make a beating sound	Patpataunu
To make a noise	Chhachalkinu
To make an incision	Pachhnu
To make bread	Patharnu
To make bright	Ujilyaunu
To make doubly sure	Khoryaunu
To make eat	Khwaunu
To make empty	Rittyaunu
To make even or smooth	Sammyaunu
To make good use of	Sumarnu
To make mention of	Ullekh
To make or sit down violently	Thacharnu
To make payment	Bujhaunu
To make run	Daudaunu
To make triple	Tebryaunu
To make use of	Behornu
To make	Tulyaunu
To mix well	Phitnu
To move briskly	Sarsaraunu
To move	Chalmalaunu, Chalnu

178

To multiply	Gunnu
To murmur	Badbadaunu
To mutter repeatedly	Japnu
To mutter	Bhunbhunaunu
To neigh	Hinhinaunu
To nourish	Posnu
To obey	Ternu, Mannu
To obstruct	Bitholnu
To occur	Sujhnu
To offer	Takryaunu
To overeat	Dhokryaunu
To overtake	Uchhinnu, Ogatnu
To palpitate	Dhadkanu, Dhamkanu
To pant	Haafnu
To pass over	Tarnu
To pass the limits of decorum	Chhihilinu
To pass	Bitaunu
To pay	Tirnu
To peck	Thugnu
To peel	Khurkanu, Chhilkanu
To peep into	Chyaunu, Jhaaknu
To penetrate	Gadnu
To persuade	Phakaunu
To pierce slightly	Bijhaunu
To pierce	Chhirnu
To pilfer	Tapkaunu
To pinch	Chimotnu
To place across	Tersyaunu
To please	Rejhaunu
To plunder	Harnu
To point by the finger	Aulyaunu
To poke	Ghochnu

179

To polish	Ghotnu, Majhnu
To ponder	Ghorinu
To pour out in small quantity	Turkyaunu
To praise	Sarhaunu
To prate in wrath	Jarkanu
To prattle	Pakbakaunu
To pray for	Bhajnu
To press for payment	Dhadnu
To press into	Dhasaunu
To print	Chhapnu
To produce a hissing sound	Phuknu
To promie to do such thing	Bhaknu
To prove	Khutyaunu, Thahryaunu
To puddle up	Hilyaunu
To pull on	Khepnu
To pull out forcibly	Jhatkarnu
To pull roughly	Ghichchyaunu
To pull up	Ukhelnu
To purify	Suddhyaunu
To pursue	Lagarnu
To put aside	Thankyaunu
To put in writing	Darnu
To put into a bag	Thailyaunu
To put on airs	Gadkanu, Gamkanu
To put	Rakhnu
To quilt	Tagnu
To rain in torrents	Darkanu
To raise	Ukasnu, Uchalnu
To reach	Pugnu
To read	Padhnu
To rebuke	Jhaparnu, Hapkaunu

To recover from illness	Tangrinu
To reform	Sudharnu
To reject	Latarnu
To release	Chhadnu
To remain	Rahanu
To repeat (words)	Udkanu
To repeat	Ratnu, Chukchukaunu, Pachhutaunu
To reproach	Thurnu, Hakarnu
To restore to life again	Jilaunu
To rinse the mouth	Khokalnu
To rip up	Ugharnu
To rise	Uthnu, Udaunu, Jhulkanu
To roam	Ghumnu
To roar	Gadgadaunu, Garjanu
To roll in the body	Lutaputinu
To roll	Gudnu, Gurrinu
To rot away	Makaunu
To row	Khiyaunu
To saunter	Larkharinu
To say	Bataunu
To scamper	Kudnu
To scare away	Bhadkaunu
To scatter on	Chhidkanu
To scent	Sughnu
To scrape	Khosyaunu
To scratch with the nails	Kotranu
To scratch	Kanyaunu, Chithornu, Daharyaunu, Phaharaunu

To scream	Chichchyaunu
To send for	Jhikaunu
To send	Pathaunu
To separate	Phattaunu
To set aloof	Parsarnu
To set fire to	Salkaunu
To set in motion	Hilaunu
To set	Jadnu
To sew thick	Autarnu
To shake greatly	Machchanu
To shape into a tube	Dhungryaunu
To sharpen	Tikharnu
To shave	Khauranu
To shear	Katranu
To shell	Chhodaunu
To shift	Osarnu
To shine	Chamkanu,
	Jagamagaunu,
	Jhalkanu
To shiver	Kaapnu
To show anger	Thaskanu
To shrink from	Hachkanu
To sift	Kelaunu
To sleep	Sutnu
To slip away	Satkanu
To slip	Chiplinu, Radkanu
To smear	Lipnu, Lesnu
To snap	Chudalnu
To snatch by force	Ruthnu
To sneeze	Chhinknu
To soak	Bhijaunu, Sosnu
To sow	Ropnu
To speak aloud	Kadkanu
To speak touching to the raw	Karetnu

182

To speak with hesitation	Kannu
To specify	Kitnu
To spill	Dholnu
To spin	Katnu
To splash with mud	Thoparnu
To splash	Chhyapnu
To split	Chirnu
To spoil	Bigranu
To spread out	Phinjaunu
To spread	Ochhyaunu, Phailinu
To spring up	Umranu
To sprinkle powdered	Burkaunu
To sprinkle	Chharkanu
To sprout	Tusaunu
To squeeze	Nimothnu
To stagger	Dharmaraunu
To stammer	Bhakbhakaunu
To stand proudly	Datnu
To stand	Ubhinu
To startle	Jhaskaunu
To stick	Tasnu
To stink	Ganhaunu
To stitch closely	Khutnu
To stool	Hagnu
To stop a hole	Rasaunu
To store	Saachnu
To strike	Bajnu, Hannu
To strike out	Keraunu
To string (flower etc)	Gaathnu
To stroke	Sumsumyaunu
To suit	Suhaunu
To sulk	Ghossinu
To support	Dhannu

183

To surround	Ghernu
To suspect	Khatkanu
To swallow	Nilnu
To swarm	Dhurinu
To sweep	Badharnu
To swerve	Dagnu
To take a task	Chhasnu
To take away	Lanu, Laijanu
To take by force	Gaajnu
To take care	Syaharnu
To take off	Utarnu
To take one across	Tarnu
To take out of the pot	Paskanu
To take out	Odarnu
To take permission	Sadhnu
To take support on head	Mantinu
To take support on	Teknu
To take	Linu
To talk irritably	Jharkanu
To talk shamelessly	Gijinu
To teach	Sikaunu
To tear hair out	Jagaltyaunu
To tear	Chyatnu
To tease	Pirnu
To tell lies	Chhakaunu
To tempt	Kalpaunu, Lobhyaunu
To that extent	Usto
To the best of one's ability	Sakesamma
To thin out (vegetables)	Bedhaunu
To think	Chitaunu, Sochɪ Unnu
To threaten	Daatnu, Dhamkaunu

To throw out by neck	Mantyaunu
To thrust by the neck	Ghokryaunu
To thrust in	Dhoknu
To thrust	Dhasnu
To tighten up a loop	Surkaunu
To tighten	Jakadnu,
	Tankaunu
To titillate	Kutkutyaunu
To trace	Pahilyaunu
To tremble	Dagdagaunu
To triplicate	Tehryaunu
To turn out	Nikalnu
To twitch	Pharpharaunu
To uproot	Ukhadnu
To urge on	Hikaunu
To urinate (of a cow)	Gautyaunu
To use harsh language	Thukranu
To vomit	Chhadnu
To wade	Helinu
To walk hither and thither	Chaharnu
To walk proudly	Tankanu
To walk slowly	Dhalkanu
To walk with quick paces	Tadkanu, Tarkanu,
	Lamkanu
To ward off	Manchhanu
To warm	Garmaunu,
	Tataunu
To wash hands and	
mouth after eating	Chuthnu
To wear out	Thotrinu
To wear shame	Lajaunu
To weed and dig round plants	Godnu
To weigh	Jokhnnu, Taulanu
To welter	Ludabudinu

To whistle	Suselnu
To winnow	Nifannu
To wring	Nichornu
To write	Likhnu
To yoke an oxen	Narnu
To-day	Aja
Toad	Bato
Tobacco	Tamakhu
Together with	Sahit
Together	Sagai, Satha
Tom-tom	Madal
Tomato	Golbhinda
Tomorrow	Bholi
Tongs	Chimta
Tongue of a bell	Ralo
Tongue of flame	Raako
Tongue	Jibhro
Too much	Ati
Tool	Hatiyar, Jyabhal
Tooth-paste	Mise
Tooth	Thote, Daat
Top secret	Nigudh
Top	Chuchuro, Bhurun, Shikhara
Topaz	Pokharaj
Topsy turvy	Ultapulta
Torch	Masal
Torn	Phatta
Tortoise	Kachhuwa, Thotare
Torture	Yatana
Total absence	Nimityanna
Total eclipse	Khagras

Total	Ekattha, Jod, Yogafal
Totality	Purnata
Totally ignorant	Patmurkha
Touch-stone	Kase
Touch	Sparsha, Chhunu
Touching	Chhutchhat
Tough fruit skin	Bokro
Tough	Chamro
Tourism	Paryatan
Towards	Taraf, Patti
Towel	Tauliya
Town	Pur
Toy	Khelauna
Trace	Atto-patto, Suinko
Tradition	Sanatn
Traditional custom	Budhe-rudhi
Traditional payment	Daidastur
Traditional	Pauranik
Tragedy	Dukhant
Train	Rela
Training	Talem
Trammels	Phashto
Trample	Kulchanu
Trance	Tandra
Transaction bond	Tamsuk
Translation	Anuwad, Ultha
Transparent	Chharlanga
Transplanting	Ropai
Transportation	Parwahan, Yatayata
Trap	Khor
Traveller	Batuwa, Musafir
Travelling	Bhraman

Tray	Kisti
Treacherous	Dagabaj
Treachery	Daga, Dagabaje
Treasurer	Tahabeldar, Bhandare
Tree	Rukha, Wriksha
Trembling	Dagmag, Tharhare, Phirphire
Trick	Kapat, Jalsaje
Trident	Trushul
Trip up	Lotaunu
Trip	Khep, Yatra
Trot	Dulki
Trotting	Dulki
Trouble	Janjal, Jhanjhat, Taklef
Troublesome	Piraha
Trousers	Patlun, Suruwala
Throw	Halnu, Phalnu
Trowel	Thurpe
Truce	Sulaha
True to one's salt	Nimkhalal
True	Sat, Sachcha, Saacho
Truely	Saachchai
Trumpet	Turhe
Trun	Bare
Trunk	Gind, Sund
Trust	Guthe, Dharot
Trustworthy	Wishwasaneya
Trusty	Jimmawal
Truth	Satya
Truthful	Satyawade

188

Truthfulness	Satyata
Tube	Dhungre
Tuesday	Mangal
Tuft of hair	Tupe
Tumbler	Aamkhoraa
Tumultuous crowd	Dangal
Tune	Tan
Tunnel	Surun
Turban	Pagare, Pheta , Safa
Turmeric	Besar
Turn round	Pharkaunu
Turn tail	Kulelamthoknu
Turn upside down	Paltanu
Turn	Alopalo, Modnu, Palat, Phera
Turned away	Wimukha
Turnip	Salagam
Tusk	Daro
Tusked	Dare
Twang of a bow	Tankar
Twelve	Bara
Twenty	Bes
Twenty-one	Ekkaes
Twenty-two	Baaes
Twenty three	Teis
Twenty-four	Chaubes
Twenty-five	Pachches
Twenty-six	Chhabbes
Twenty-seven	Sattaisa
Twenty-eight	Atthais
Twenty-eight stars	Nakshatra
Twenty-nine	Unantees
Twig used for cleaning teeth	Datiwan

189

Twin	Jumlyaha, Nimesh
Twist	Batnu
Twisting	Bhanjo
Two and half	Adhaai
Two anna-bit	Duanne
Two legged	Duikhutte, Dopaya
Two miles	Kos
Two ounces	Chhatak
Two-storeyed	Duitale
Two	Dui
Twofold	Duiguna
Tyranny	Atyaachar
Ugliness	Bhaddapan
Ugly lips	Othe
Ugly	Bhadda
Ulcer	Phoda
Umbrella	Chhata
Un-essential	Bokre
Unaccountable	Behisab
Unapproachable	Agam
Unauspiciousness	Bichchhuk
Unbearable heat	Ukharmaulo
Unbearable	Akhaanu, Asaihya
Unbleached cloth	Markin
Unbroken continuation	Bistur
Unbroken	Atut
Uncastrated animal	Saadh
Unchaste woman	Rande
Unchaste	Kulta
Unchecked	Nirwighna
Uncivil	Beadab
Unclaimed	Bewares
Uncle	Kaka
Unclean	Aghore

Uncombed hair	Jhaakro
Uncommon	Bechalte, Wilakshana
Unconscious	Behosh, Murchhit
Uncover	Ugharnu
Uncultivated	Parta
Under jacket	Bhoto
Under one's control	Swayatta
Under one's very nose	Dekhadekhe
Under the eyes of	Sakshat
Under	Tallo
Understand	Jannu
Understanding	Dujli
Understood	Wigyaata, Samjhinu
Underworld	Rasatal
Undeveloped	Awiksit
Undivided	Sagola
Undivisible	Akhand
Uneducated	Apadh, Nirakshar, Beilame
Unemployed	Dhakre, Bekam, Bekar
Unemployment	Bekare
Unexpectedly	Jhapjhuppa, Tuplukka
Unfit	Anuchit, Ayogya
Ungrateful	Kritaghna, Nikakharam
Unhappiness	Bemajja
Unhappy	Dukhe
Uniform	Jangeposhak, Bana
Uninformed	Bekhabar
Unintelligent	Paddhu

191

Unintelligible language	Gathyanguthun
Union	Yojana
Unique	Adwiteya
United	Sanyukta
Unity	Ekta, Gath, Mel
Universal monarch	Chakrawarte
Universe	Wishwa
University	Wishwawidyalaya
Unjust person	Anyaaye
Unknowing	Anjaan
Unlawful	Najayaj, Bejabta
Unlimited	Behad
Unlucky	Bhagyahen
Unmanageable work	Jhonj
Unmanly	Lote
Unmanned	Bharanga
Unmarried	Lyaite
Unmarried girl	Kanya
Unmarried wife	Lakhaute
Unmixed	Wishuddha
Unnatural	Aswabhawik
Unnecessary obstinacy	Bidhanga
Unproductive land	Banjar
Unrestrained	Nirankush
Unripe	Kaacho
Unserviceable	Bekamma
Unsociable	Amildo
Unsteady	Wichalit
Unsuitable time	Kubela
Untie	Phukaunu
Untouchable	Achhute
Unused	Kora
Unusual	Bedhab
Unusually	Satara

Unwell	Madhauru
Unwholesome	Kupathya
Unworthy son	Kaput
Unyielding	Chaparchand, Jhakkad
Up to this time	Yatinjel
Upper class	Raithane
Upper	Upallo, Mathillo
Upside-down	Ulatpalat
Upto	Tak
Urinal	Pishabkhana
Urinate through fear	Chhulchhulyaunu
Urine	Pishab, Mut
Use	Upayog, Chalte
Useless boast	Gudde
Useless talk	Badbad
Useless	Ulfat, Phajul, Phosro, Radde, Lakhane, Wahiyata, Silpat
Uselessly	Phwaak, Mafat
Usual	Wyawaharik
Usufructuary mortgage	Bhogbandhak
Utensil	Bartan
Uterine	Sahodar
Utmost endeavour	Dhun
Uvula	Ligalige
Vacancy	Khalekhalsa
Vaccinate	Khopnu
Vagabond	Dulante
Vagary	Manmoj
Vain	Writha
Valley	Upatyaka
Valuable	Bahumulya

Value	Kadar
Vanish	Wailaunu
Vanity	Mapaen
Vapour	Baf
Varnish	Barnish, Rogana
Vegetable garden	Bare
Vegetable	Tarkare, Wanaspati, Sag
Vehicle of Gods	Ratha
Vein	Naso
Velvet	Makhmal
Verdigris	Ugal
Verification	Ruju, Tahakekat
Vermillion-coloured	Sindure
Vermillion	Singraf, Sindur
Verse	Chhand
Vertebrate	Merudande
Very dreadful	Mahaghor
Very eager for	Lolupa
Very harsh	Nadirshahe
Very lean (female)	Sitthe
Very lean (male)	Sittha
Very much	Audhe, Chaupatta, Nikai, Besare, Lattekutte, Sarhai
Very slowly	Bistarai
Very sly	Chhattesa
Very tall and fat	Dhaddu
Very thick	Pragadh
Vessel	Bhaado, Wartana
Vest	Ganje
Vexation	Jharko, Tanga
Victorious	Wijaye
Victory	Jaya, Wijaya

Vigil	Jagram
Vigorous	Jabardast
Village	Gau, Dehat, Baste
Villager	Gaule
Vine	Belo
Violence	Prachandata, Lutapeta, Lutamara
Virility	Paurakh
Virtuous conduct	Sadachar
Virtuous	Gune, Dharmashel, Sadacharc
Visit	Bhctghat
Vitality	Sattwa
Vituperation	Utarne
Vocabulary	Shabdasangraha
Voice	Awaj, Wane, Swar
Volcano	Jwalamukhe
Voluntary work	Shramadana
Volunteer	Swayamsewak
Voluptuary	Bhogwilase
Vomit	Ukelnu, Wakka
Vomitting	Wamana, Wanta
Voracious	Hantakale
Vulgar	Pakhe
Vulture	Giddha
Vulva	Pute
Wages	Nimek, Wetan
Waist-belt	Kammarbande
Waist	Kammar
Waiting for a thing	Prateksha
Wakeful	Jaga
Waking moments	Wipana

Walk	Tahalnu, Dulna, Hindna
Walking round	Pradakshina
Walking	Hinddul
Wall screen	Bhet
Wall	Garo, Parkhal, Bhitto
Wallet	Jabe
Walnut	Okhar
Wandering through countries	Deshatan
Wandering	Wihar
Want of proper care	Bisyahar
Want	Khatta, Chahanu
War	Janga, Rana
Warning	Janau
Warrant	Sanad
Warrior	Ladaka
Wart	Muso
Wary	Battesa
Wash	Dhunu, Pakhalnu
Washerman	Dhobe
Washerwoman	Dhobine
Wasp	Barud
Waste away	Makinu
Waste	Ujad, Khera, Parte
Watch	Rakhaware
Watchful	Khabardar
Watchman	Pale, Rakhawala
Water course	Dhara
Water reed	Kaash
Water-chestnut	Singada
Water-mill	Ghatta
Water-pot	Kamandalu, Ghat

Water-weed	Sinwale
Water	Jala, Pane, Hite
Waterfall	Chhaharo
Watering in field	Patai
Waterpot with holes	Jhaajar
Wave of water	Tarang
Wave	Chhal, Lahare
Wax	Main
Way	Path
We	Hame
Weak	Kamjor, Durbal, Najor, Nirdho, Phitalo, Lukhure
Weakness	Natakat
Wealth and property	Dhansampatti
Wealth	Aishwarya, Daulat, Puje, Paisa, Lakshme, Waibhawa, Sampatti
Wealthy	Dhanadhya, Waibhawashale
Weapon	Astra, Shastra, Hathatiyar
Weapons and uniforms	Tanamana
Weariness	Thakai, Pattai
Wearing	Lawai
Weather	Mausam
Weave	Bunnu
Weaver	Julaha
Weaving	Bunawat
Web	Jalo
Wednesday	Budhabar
Weed	Mothe

Weedy	Chamero
Week	Saptaha, Sata, Hapta
Weekly market	Pithiyaa
Weeping	Ruwawase, Wilapa
Weeping-face	Pilpilaaudo
Weight	Taul, Wajana
Weights and measures	Dhak
Weighty	Bhare, Swagat
Welfare	Kalyan, Bhalai, Bhalo
Well cooked meat	Pakku
Well done	Syabas
Well looked after	Pushta
Well-adorned	Sushobhit
Well-fed	Bharilo
Well-known	Suprashiddha
Well-versed	Khaggad
Well-wisher	Hitkare, Hitchintak, Hitaishe
Well-wishing	Hitchitan
Well	Kuwa, Khub, Niko, Ramrare
West	Pachchhim
Wetnurse	Bubu
What is left	Rahakula
Whatsoever	Jastosukai, Jesukai
Wheat-stalk	Chhwale
Wheat	Gahu
Wheedling	Lolopoto
Wheel	Chakra, Pahiya, Pangro, Paiaa
Wheeled	Pangre

198

When	Kahile, Jaba
Where	Kahaa
Wheresoever	Jahaasukai
Wherever	Jatasukai, Jahaa
Wherstone	Sile
Which	Jun
Whichever	Kastai, Junsukai
Whiplash	Chabuk
Whipping	Korra
Whirlpool	Bhumare
Whisper	Kanekhuse
Whistle	Sete
White cloth	Nainsut
White horse	Sabja
White leprosy	Dubhe
White	Safeda, Seto
Whither	Kata, Jata
Whitish in complexion	Gahu-goro
Whole-hearted	Manoman
Whole	Jamma, Samasta, Singo
Wholesale trader	Kothewal
Wholly	Sampurnataya
Whore-monger	Bhaad
Why	Kina
Wicked-fellow	Durjan
Wicked	Badmash, Haram
Wickedness	Badmashe
Wicker basket	Doko
Wide open space	Phaat
Wide-spread	Byapta, Wyapaka
Wide	Chaklo, Chauda, Pharakilo
Wideness	Wyapakata

Widow	Raade, Widhawa
Widower	Raado
Wife of cupid	Rati
Wife of a gardener	Maline
Wife of elder brother	Bhauju
Wife of husband's younger brother	Dewarane
Wife's elder brother	Jethan
Wife	Joe, Patne, Swasne
Wild buffalo	Arnaa
Wild pigeon	Malewa
Wild	Jangale
Wilful	Swechchhachare
Willing & glad	Rajekhushe
Willy-nilly	Rajewiraje
Wily	Jale
Winding river	Jaghar
Window-bar	Dadalne
Window	Khidke, Jhyal, Sanjhyal
Windy	Batase
Wine shop	Bhatte
Wine	Madira, Mat, Mad
Wing	Pakheta, Pankha, Pwaakh
Winking of the eye	Pala
Winning	Jit
Winter	Jado, Hiud
Wipe out	Metnu
Wire	Tar
Wise	Wigya
Wish	Abhilaasha, Manakanchhe
Wished for	Manchinte

200

Witch	Daine, Bokse
With a flare	Dandan
With a jerk	Thwatta, Hutta
With a swish	Hurra
With child	Dojiya
With joy	Masta
With no trouble at all	Sitimite
With	Sita
Without a settled ending	Bhasbhus
Without blemish	Nikhara
Without cause	Akaran, Nahak
Without excuse	Niruttar
Without food	Nirahar
Without juice	Beras
Without pause	Sarasar
Without price	Bedam
Without purpose	Wyartha
Without qualities	Nirgun
Without spot	Bedag
Without stopping	Danadan
Without water	Nirjal
Without	Bina, Wina
Witness	Sakshe
Wizard	Tunyaha, Bokso
Woeful	Shokakula
Wolf	Hudar
Woman in her period	Rajaswala, Rajowate
Woman	Nare
Womb	Kokha, Patheghar
Women	Aimac
Wonder	Udek, Chakit, Chhakka, Tajub
Wonderful	Gajab

Wood shop	Kathmahal
Wood	Kath, Lakade
Woodcutter	Daure
Wood log	Mudho
Wooden board	Pate
Wooden bridge	Saaghu
Wooden cask	Pham
Wooden pitcher	Theke
Wooden screen	Kathbar
Wooden seat	Pira
Wooden support for climbing plants	Thangro
Wooden vessel	Sinman, Harpe
Woodpecker	Lahaache
Wool	Un
Woollen blanket	Rade
Woollen mantle	Mande
Woollen shawl	Dhussa
Woollen stocking	Docha
Woollen-blanket	Kamlo
Woollen cloth	Pattu
Woollen	Une
Word of honour	Eman-Jaman
Word	Shabda
Wordly	Sansare
Words spoken in anger	Kadkakadke
Wordy dispute	Bhanawaire
Work	Kam
Worker of lac	Lahate
Worker	Kamdar
Working up of loss	Bejo
World	Jagat, Brahmanda, Loka, Sansar, Chinta

Worry	Jhijo, Phikre
Worship	Aaraadhan, Puja, Wandana
Worshipper	Pujare
Worth studying	Pathya
Worthless	Nikamma, Patru, Phogatiya
Worthy of worship	Pujya
Worthy person	Patra, Supatra
Wothy of praise	Prashansaneya
Would-be	Bhawe
Wound	Ghau, Chot, Danak
Wounded	Ghayal
Wrangling and fighting	Ladantabhidanta
Wrap up	Bernu
Wrapped	Liptinu
Wrapper	Aachal, Bethan
Wrestler	Pahalwan
Wrestling	Dwandayuddha, Kustaa-Kusti
Wrinkle	Chaure
Wristlet	Baju
Writer	Raitar, Lekhaka
Writing	Likhata, Lekhai
Written by hand	Hastalikhit
Written confession	Jamanbande
Written document	Lekhota, Manjurnaamaa
Written paper	Parcha
Written	Likhita
Wrong course	Kubato
Wrung	Nichorina
Yak	Chaure

Yam	Tarul
Yama	Yama
Yarn	Sut
Year	Warsha, Sal, Samwatsar
Years old almanac	Bele
Yellow colour	Wasante
Yellow pigment	Rochana
Yellowish	Besare
Yes	Ha
Yesterday	Hijo
Yet growing	Bharkharko
Yielding much milk	Dudhahar
Yogi	Awadhut
Young (fem)	Tarune
Young (masc)	Taruno
Young camel	Bota
Young girl	Bala
Young lady	Yuwate
Young man	Gabdu, Nawayuwak, Baraath
Young women	Baraathinu
Young	Jawan, Tannere, Naujawan, Yuwa
Younger sister	Bahine
Youngest	Kanchha
Your good self	Tapain
Yours faithfully	Bhawadeya
Youth-club	Yuwaka-sangha
Youth	Pattho, Yuwaka, Yauwana
Zero	Shunya
Zircon	Gomed
Zoo	Chidiyaghar